HOW TO GET
RICH, POWERFUL,
HEALTHY AND SEXY
WHILE YOU WAIT

HOW TO GET RICH, POWERFUL, HEALTHY AND SEXY
WHILE YOU WAIT

ELEANOR ROWE
ILLUSTRATED BY JACK ZIEGLER

HOW TO GET
RICH, POWERFUL,
HEALTHY AND SEXY
WHILE YOU WAIT

Copyright © 2012 by Eleanor Rowe

BOOK DESIGN AND PRODUCTION:
Jane Perini, Thunder Mountain Design
www.thundermountaindesign.com

ISBN 13: 978-0-615-57720-3

FOR WOODY

CONTENTS

....

INTRODUCTION

....

COMPANY PRESIDENTS DO IT. Boarding-house residents do it.
Musicians and magicians do it. Everybody waits. We spend one-
tenth of our waking hours waiting, according to Dr. Thomas L. Satyr,
an expert on the branch of applied mathematics that deals with
waiting lines.

Most of us dislike waiting. It can be annoying, frustrating, even
exhausting. The solution? Become a master instead of a victim of
waiting situations. Use time you might otherwise waste for goals
you might otherwise not achieve. Be prepared for waiting—and turn
irritation into pleasure, accomplishment, and satisfaction.

What are your goals? Whether they involve money, health, power,
appearance, or personal relationships, this book can help you achieve
them. You will find ways to increase your energy, improve your face and
figure, and reduce stress. There are also suggested methods for drawing
upon and coordinating the power of your mind and emotions. All this
can be done while you wait.

ACKNOWLEDGMENTS

·····························

M ANY SPECIAL PEOPLE helped shape this book and I owe them much. My agent, Ann Buchwald, contributed just the right criticism, insight, and encouragement. Shelley Liebman, director of The Home Stretch, a creative fitness program, gave valuable advice on many of the exercises. Alexandra Gignoux, a yoga teacher who beautifully exemplifies the contemporary relevance of an ancient teaching, made helpful suggestions. The benefits of yoga are also well demonstrated by Peggy Rude, who shared valuable insights from years of teaching yoga, movement, and body-awareness. Lilias Folan, whose loving enthusiasm and expertise are known to millions of TV viewers throughout the country, gave helpful advice and encouragement. Many thanks to Ethel Golder, who gave lucid, expert suggestions. I am grateful to the Jungian analyst Suzanne Short for her insights concerning the sections dealing with the mind and the subconscious. Special thanks go to Elizabeth Nichols, Sandra Cope, Julia Gillispie, and Marilyn Langemaid. And particularly to Cynthia Rowland, whose facial exercises have helped countless women stay lovely and youthful. Instructors at various athletic clubs were also helpful, as were numerous teachers and fellow students in a great variety of self-improvement courses over many years. This book records their answers to the question: "What do you do while you wait?" My editor, John Thornton, deserves particular thanks for his perceptive help. My husband, William Woodin Rowe, provided essential aid and encouragement. Most of all, I am grateful to my spiritual teacher, Jetsunma Ahkön Lhamo.

WAITING
....
To Meet or See Someone

Avoid Nervousness

Arnold, 35, recently became a lobbyist for a major international organization. Much of his day is spent on Capitol Hill with Very Important People. While waiting to see them, he does certain exercises you can also do to Avoid Nervousness.

- Remember and re-experience moments of great personal success.
- Create within yourself positive feelings for the VIP.
- Picture in detail the meeting as you wish it to go.
- Picture the VIP in his underwear—or in her curlers and mud pack.

Benefits: *Increased confidence, poise, and personal magnetism.*

Be Impressive

Recent studies show that tall men and, to some people's surprise, tall women make considerably more money per year than their shorter peers. If you are tall, it may be easier to seem important and to be taken seriously.

Diana, 44, is very short, but you tend not to notice it. And she is taken very seriously indeed. She is one of the most successful sales representatives of a major computer firm, with a salary that runs well into six figures. When waiting to meet a potential customer, she seems to fill the room with her presence.

How does she accomplish this? She practices the following:

Stand or sit in such a way as to fill as much space as possible (within the bounds of propriety). Position your body so it appears as expanded and solid as possible. Be sure (1) your spine is erect, (2) your upper body is pulled up from the waist to your greatest height, (3) your shoulders are back and down, and (4) your legs and feet are uncrossed and set squarely on the floor. Now your body announces that you feel confident and worthy. This is the opposite of the hunched, flimsy posture of someone who is nervous or insecure.

Focus your mind completely on the present moment. Feel the appropriateness of your being there. Be conscious of your worthiness to take the time of the person you are waiting to see.

These suggestions apply particularly to the final moments of waiting to see someone important in your life.

Benefits: *You communicate that you are confident, alert, and deserve the time and space you occupy.*

NOTE: When you follow these suggestions, you are actually drawing on some ancient Eastern principles. For thousands of years, the throat has been regarded as the power center. The solar plexus (the area between the rib cage and navel) is held to be the seat of dynamic energy and vitality. According to Yogis and other masters of Eastern wisdom, when you slump and bow your head you cramp these centers and make them less effective.

Relieve Anxiety and Tension

Elmer, 50, a burly boxing commissioner, was terrified of dentists and injections. Unfortunately, years of not flossing caught up with him, and he was confronted with both. The dentist noticed his anxiety and suggested a relaxation exercise that can be done in any waiting room, The Rag Doll.

- Tense and then relax various parts of your body, starting with the feet and proceeding to calves, thighs, etc. Allow five seconds for each area.
- As you relax each body part, concentrate on the feeling of relaxation and remember it.
- As you are called from the waiting room, maintain this relaxed feeling and recreate it in any body part that is tense.

This exercise is so inconspicuous that no one around you will notice anything unusual.

Benefits: *When tension is relieved, pain is greatly diminished, energy is conserved, and the mind remains clear.*

The Rag Doll is helpful while waiting to see doctors, potential employers, or IRS auditors.

Be a Star

A famous movie actress was walking down Fifth Avenue with a friend. Her friend was amazed that no one seemed to recognize her. "All right," she said, "if you want me to look like a star, watch this!" Suddenly she was surrounded by people gawking, shoving, and asking for her autograph. She had not done anything particularly noticeable. It was more a change of bearing, a sudden, dynamic inner posture. Every atom of her body seemed to sparkle with awareness of beauty and to announce, "I'm a star!"

The key is consciousness of beauty, radiance, worth. Every woman can project "star" quality. Almost every bride does. "All brides are beautiful" is a rule proven by very few exceptions. If you have ever felt radiantly beautiful and particularly worthy and special, you can do it again, at will. Here is how:

- Recall such moments from your past and vividly re-experience them. Become momentarily absorbed in the feelings you had then. Remember particularly the times that someone thought you were terrific.
- Visualize a radiant sun in your solar plexus (the area between your rib cage and your navel).

* Feel glowing energy bursting through every cell of your body, energizing every atom, bringing a radiant glow to your face.

As you wait to make an entrance or to meet someone, be aware that you are a unique and special human being, the successful star in the drama of your life.

Benefits: *You radiate energy and allow your true beauty to shine. As you feel the positive response of others, your self-image blossoms.*

Project a Dynamic Attractiveness

Doris, 38, a psychologist, wouldn't win any beauty contests. She has irregular, unremarkable features, and her figure has several flaws. Yet people describe her as "stunning" and "truly beautiful." Men are continually falling in love with her, and she is always surrounded at a party.

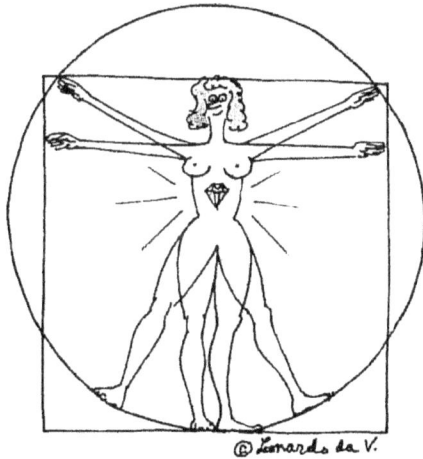

© Leonardo da V.

Once, during a discussion of beauty, she remarked, "It's a matter of loving yourself. It's an inner bearing, as if you carried a jewel at the center of your being. You are fully aware of its value and its radiance, and you willingly share your joy in it with others."

Doris did not have Eastern teachings in mind, but her comments—
when seen in their light—lead to a subtle exercise in consciousness.
This exercise is particularly useful while waiting to be introduced to an
individual, a group, or an audience.

- Imagining a jewel in your solar plexus aptly suggests the center
  of radiance in your body.

- Focusing on this image in this center increases the vitality
  and power of your personality. (This sets you apart from most
  people, who scatter their energies and their impact, whose
  emotions are a tangle, and whose thoughts are undirected.)

- Dynamism and the impact of your personality result from
  functioning as a unified, integrated being. All mental and
  emotional energies are aimed in the same direction or
  concentrated on the same object.

Benefits: *Your personality becomes more vibrant and dynamic.
People are drawn to you in a positive way. You attain a quality or a
bearing that could be described as "regal." It becomes easier to draw
yourself up from the waist and maintain good posture.*

Achieve a Healthy Glow

Gwen, 39, is recently divorced and very popular. While waiting for a
date to arrive, she does the Natural Blush.

- Bend from the waist, hanging your upper body loosely toward
  the floor.

■ Stay that way for a few moments; then come up slowly, uncurling the spine one vertebra at a time.

This is also good to do while waiting to have your picture taken. And of course, you can save on rouge.

Benefits: *A vibrant, healthy glow on your face. As yoga students know, the complexion improves from reversals of the pull of gravity. This exercise also releases pressure on the lower back.*

NOTE: In this position you can gently but firmly pat your face to bring more circulation and glow to your complexion. One woman who is still lovely at 79 has been doing it for fifty years, every morning and before every important occasion. Knowing she looks wonderful helps to give her the energy to continue an active life. It is good to do this exercise after you have washed and moisturized your face. Be careful not to stretch or pull the skin.

Meet the Right Person

Mary Jane, 29 ½, wanted to be loved. She was desperately Waiting for the Right Man to come along. Men seemed to sense her longing and stayed away in droves. To fill up lonely evenings, she signed up for a course in Greek drama. She was struck by the wisdom of the ancients' belief that "character is destiny," and decided to change hers. She stopped thinking about her own needs and pains and focused upon self-improvement and concern for others. She worked on her appearance and self-image and became more loving and giving. Her life became so full that she decided she no longer needed a man to give it meaning. Then, of course, they came running.

- Start an exercise program.
- Become a good listener.
- Do some volunteer-work.
- Follow the ancient advice, "Know thyself," and find the strength within.

If you are waiting to have someone else take care of your needs, forget it! The quality of those around you is a reflection of what you are. If you wish to attract a special person, make yourself more worthy.

Benefits: *Life will provide all the blessings you have stopped chasing.*

WAITING

....

In Line

Enlarge Your Social Life

Peter, 25, a bachelor, fresh out of law school and new in town, quickly
determined that all the women in his firm were either married or
decidedly uninteresting. He began to devote all his spare time and
energy to making new friends. As resourceful at play as at work, he
devised a system for exploiting the possibilities of waiting moments.

For grocery stores:

- Choose a store where suitable singles are likely to shop.

- Be aware of the other shoppers as you go through the aisles.
  People who choose frozen dinners-for-one are likely to be
  unattached. If you are inclined to gourmet cooking—or eating—
  linger near such items.

- Choose to wait in the check-out line behind the most attractive
  prospect you have spotted.

- A question about an item in someone's cart often evokes
  helpful answers—and can lead to much more. "How do you
  cook those?" can be the seed from which romance or friendship
  sprouts, and so can "Does your cat really like that stuff?"

Women usually enjoy giving advice about food. Questions about a pet can open conversational—and other—doors.

For bookstores:

- Linger near the sections of books in which you have a special interest or expertise. You may have an opportunity to be helpful—and appear authoritative. ("That's a good book, but not as reliable as this one.")

- Browse near the bestsellers. Singles who buy them often have the leisure and inclination for conversation.

- It's helpful to be prepared if you linger—to have read at least some of the important reviews. The sexual revolution and the women's movement notwithstanding, most women still appreciate an informed and authoritative male mind.

- Browse near the check-out, and get in line behind the most interesting prospect. The books that have been selected will suggest a handy conversation opener. "That looks interesting" can lead to something really interesting.

Benefits: *Fun and adventure are added to shopping trips. Possibly new friendships and even romance will result.*

Keep Your Body in Line

Isabel, 37, wife of an American diplomat in Soviet Moscow, could have done all her shopping at the hard-currency stores that existed especially for foreigners. But she wanted to practice her Russian and to understand how Russian women really lived. She discovered that there

were no supermarkets—each type of food had its own store—and that
waiting in line was a major Russian occupation. First you get in line to
select your item; you get in another line to pay for it; then you get in
a third line to pick it up. And the lines were long. The shoppers were
mostly women—on whom a diet largely of bread and potatoes had left
its mark. Most seemed agelessly old and formlessly fat.

Isabel was inspired to shape up her own body, and to exercise as
much as possible—unobserved—while standing in line. She found
that she tired more when she slumped, so she worked on her posture.
She kept her upper body pulled up from her breast bone, her shoulders
down and back, and her head right on top of her shoulders rather than
protruding forward. Here is an exercise that helped her to achieve this
alignment:

1. Pretend that you are standing against a wall. Slide your back down a few inches as you bend your knees. Maintain a strong vertical alignment of your torso and head as you do this.

2. In this position, pull your shoulders back, as if trying to make your shoulder blades touch. Hold for a moment and release.

3. Take a deep breath into your abdomen. As you exhale, press your abdominal muscles tightly against your spine. Hold for several seconds.

4. After getting used to this position, you can make it harder by lifting your heels off the ground and lowering your body a little more.

An exercise for the neck: Without moving your body, turn your head as far as possible right and left. (In Soviet Russia, this was a good way to check if you were being followed.)

An exercise for the waist: Without moving your lower body, turn your upper body as far as possible right and left. (It will appear that you are looking for someone.)

Isometric exercises, to be held for several seconds:

- Tighten your seat muscles. (Pretend that there is a dime between your buttocks and you want to keep it from slipping.)

- Press your thighs together as tightly as possible.

- Clasp or hook your hands together in front of your chest. Press them together; then try to pull them apart.

- Clasp your hands behind your buttocks. Pull down from your shoulders. This makes your upper back arch slightly.

Benefits: *Your posture and figure improve. The movement is good for your circulation, keeps you warmer in winter, and is ultimately less tiring than simply standing. Boredom and impatience can be exhausting.*

Exercise Your Hands and Feet

Catherine, 50, an engineer, goes to all the new movies as soon as they open. While waiting in the ticket line, she does a variety of hand and foot exercises.

The Wrist Wriggle:

- Make fists; then spread fingers wide.
- Rotate wrists in both directions.
- Flex your wrists up and down.
- Shake your hands out loosely.

Benefits: *Improves circulation, as well as the flexibility and strength of hands and wrists. Helpful for racquet sports and golf.*

The Rock, Roll and Rise:

- Roll slowly forward onto toes, then back onto heels.
- Roll weight onto outside of feet and curl toes down.
- Roll weight onto inside of feet, curling toes up.

Benefits: *Improves strength, flexibility, and coordination of the legs and feet. Good for circulation.*

WAITING
....
On the Telephone

Prepare to Shop by Phone

Mabel, 44, a sales representative who works out of her own home, is continually left Waiting on Hold. She keeps catalogues by the phone, along with her shopping lists and credit card numbers.

She browses through the catalogues while on hold and then is ready to do her shopping by phone.

Benefits: You shop more efficiently and avoid irritation while on hold.

Hold the Line for Fitness

Gretchen, 35, administrative assistant to a university president, spends hours on the phone in the school's ongoing fundraising effort. Her evenings are taken up by three teenagers—and by college classes. Her time at the telephone is her time for fitness. This is what she does:

Weight exercises with her free arm (when she first started these, she lifted either the telephone, a heavy paperweight, or the phone book; now she keeps a three-pound weight in her drawer.) Do these while seated in your chair. Do only a few repetitions at first. Gradually increase the number of repetitions and the heaviness of the weight. Start each exercise with the weight held at your chest.

1. Lift the weight straight up to the ceiling; then bring it down behind your head as far as you can comfortably reach.

2. Swing it out directly to the side; then make several arm circles with it forward, then backward.

3. Swing it out directly to the side, then forward to touch your chest.

4. Slowly lower it sideways and touch the floor with it about a foot from your chair.

Isometrics (to be held several seconds):

1. While sitting, tighten your seat muscles and press your knees together.

2. Tighten your abdominal muscles and draw them in toward your spine.

3. Press with your free arm under your desk, as if trying to lift it.

Under-desk leg extensions:

1. Tightening your abdominals as you sit, stretch one leg at a time horizontally in front of you.

2. In this position, move it up and down several inches.

3. Holding on to the desk top and tightening your abdominals, stretch both legs horizontally in front of you.

Be sure to exercise both sides of your body.

Benefits: *Overall conditioning and toning. Frustration and irritation are replaced by a feeling of accomplishment. You can get a pretty good workout on hold.*

Make Progress on Projects

Linda, 54, secretary to a prominent socialite, makes the following suggestions for what to do when on hold:

- Buy a plastic attachment for your receiver so that it rests on your shoulder, freeing both hands.

- Keep within easy reach of the telephone:
  - Needlepoint or knitting
  - Manicure equipment
  - Magazines or other reading materials
  - Lists of vocabulary words
  - The textbook of a foreign language you wish to learn

Benefits: *You remain alert and cheerful. You accomplish something worthwhile.*

Prepare for Success

Kevin, 26, is a sales representative of a major firm manufacturing computers. Much of his contact work is done on the telephone. While trying to reach an important potential customer, he is often placed on hold. He has found two effective uses for his waiting time:

- He gives himself a pep talk: "I'm good at this. I believe in my product and know all that I need to know about it. This customer can benefit from what I have to say."

- He reviews his sales strategy, the main points of which are jotted down in front of him. Included is information about the customer's business and the ways it would profit from his product.

Benefits: *He is confident, relaxed, and fully prepared.*

Exercise Your Feet

A beauty secret of several actresses and models: while on the phone, they roll their shoeless feet on an old-style Coca Cola bottle. Its ridges are especially effective for massaging the soles of the feet. Knobbed rubber balls that kittens play with can also be used for this purpose. (You can even purchase a wooden roller made for massaging the soles in this manner.)

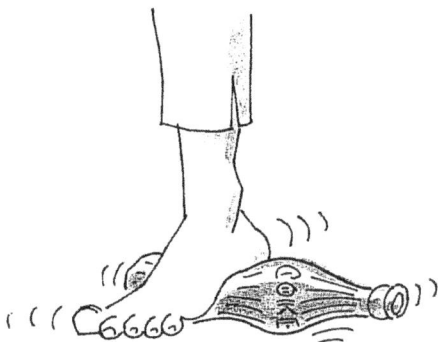

Benefits: *Exercises the feet and increases circulation. According to proponents of reflexology, stimulation of the soles is beneficial to health. The nerve endings on the bottom of the feet are related to various organs of the body. As the feet are massaged, the corresponding organs are also stimulated.*

Get in Shape for Skiing

Rudi, 33, salesman for a home-improvement firm, loves to ski. While on hold, he gets in shape for the slopes. He does the Skier's Squat.

1. Stand with your feet 3-4 inches apart, toes pointed forward.

2. Keep your back straight and heels on the floor as you bend your knees. Lower the body about 12 inches.

3. Remember to keep the knees directly over the middle toes and the weight evenly distributed on both feet.

Rudi sometimes does this exercise in front of a mirror to make sure that his knees and feet don't roll in.

A variation that will strengthen different muscles of the leg: Stand with your feet shoulder-width apart, feet turned out. (It's important to keep the knees over the feet and your back straight.)

Benefits: *Tones and strengthens the legs. It is great for the lower back and pelvic region, but be sure to keep your back straight.*

Slim and Firm Your Waist

Geraldine, 22, an actress in a daytime-television drama, does Hip Swings while on hold.

- Stand with your feet apart, knees slightly bent.
- Keeping your abdominal muscles firm, shift hips first to one side, then to the other without swaying forward or backward.

Benefits: *Slims and firms hips and waist. By improving hip flexibility, Hip Swings can also improve your walk, golf swing, skiing skill, bowling game, and lovemaking.*

Exercise Your Ankles and Toes

Young and lovely at 81, Elizabeth does foot exercises while waiting for her phone calls to go through. She moves only her toes and feet, and the dachshund sleeping on her lap is not disturbed.

- Rotate your ankles first in one direction, then in the other.
- Separate and wiggle your toes. This is best done without shoes.
- Flex and point your ankles and feet.
- Try to pick up an imaginary (or real) pencil from the floor with your toes.

Benefits: *Improves circulation and strengthens the feet. These exercises can also help to eliminate foot cramps.*

As Jean Houston said in a letter to Hints from Heloise, "You don't quit exercising when you grow old,...you grow old when you quit exercising."

Tone and Firm Your Face

Evangeline, 37, a fashion consultant, dislikes wrinkles in her clothes— and on her face. While waiting at the telephone, she does facial exercises for her mouth and cheeks. Try the "O":

1. Make a tight oval with your mouth. Attempt to close your lips over your teeth.

2. At the same time, close your eyes and raise your eyebrows.

3. Keeping your mouth tense, use your upper cheek muscles to pull the corners of your mouth into a smile.

4. Feel the tightness in the muscles of your face. Slowly relax.

You might try puffing out your cheeks as if blowing up a balloon. Hold for a few seconds and release. Some people keep bubble gum or a balloon by the telephone just for the purpose of exercising their mouth and cheek muscles.

Benefits: *Combats wrinkles around the mouth and cheeks. Tones the face.*

NOTE: The above "O" position is perfect for massaging your face. You are less likely to pull or stretch your skin.

Tone and Strengthen Your Thighs

Greg, 38, executive assistant in an insulation firm, had weak and flabby thighs when he started his job. He soon realized that the minutes he waited on hold could be used for Wall-Sitting.

1. Stand about a foot from the wall, feet pointing straight ahead.

2. Slide your back down the wall until you feel a tightness in your thighs. Pull in your abdomen as you hold this position.

3. To come out of this position, slide back up. If that is too difficult, slide down to the floor.

Eventually you will be able to sit fairly comfortably with your thighs parallel to the floor. To keep the exercise challenging, hold the position for longer and longer periods of time.

Benefits: *If you have a desk job, getting up out of your chair frequently is in itself beneficial. It helps to know that every second someone keeps you waiting, your thighs are improving. The exercise is fairly invisible—people walking by assume you are sitting on a stool. If you tighten your abdominal muscles at the same time, you make the exercise even more beneficial.*

WAITING

·····························
In a Car

Tone Your Mouth and Neck Muscles

The most basic of all measures to fight facial flab is the famous
Swedish vowel exercise.

Arthur, 53, dapper owner of a fashionable boutique, habitually does
the Vowel Howl while waiting at a red light.

■ Say the following, slowly and with as much facial exaggeration
as possible:

Benefits: Tones mouth and neck muscles.

Occasionally do the High "E" for your chin:

- Roll your tongue back, putting tip against the roof of your mouth. Sing E's as high as you can.

Benefits: *Gets rid of a double chin. Some people also claim that it improves their singing voice.*

Flatten Your Stomach

Janie, in spite of middle age, rich desserts, three children, and other blessings, has one of the flattest abdomens in town. At every red light she does the Red Squeeze.

- Pull in your abdomen and hold until the light turns green. You may wish to hold for a shorter time, especially at first.

This is best for a passenger or an experienced driver who can also keep focused on the main job of driving.

Benefits: *A flatter stomach and minimal irritation at red lights.*

Relieve a Stiff or Tense Neck

Roger, 49, head of a fast-growing advertising agency, begins his day by preparing for action. As he waits for his car to warm up, his neck gets a warm-up too.

Roll-a-Heads:

- Drop your head forward; then slowly roll it to the right, then back, then left, and again to the front.
- Keep your shoulders loose, like a jacket on a coat hanger. Roll again, reversing direction.
- Keep your body still and turn your head to the left as far as possible, then to the right.

Benefits: *In the morning, stiffness is relieved and circulation is increased. In the evening, the tensions and stresses of the day are released. Also tones the neck and controls any tendency to a double chin. According to yoga wisdom, your eyesight also improves as circulation to the eye nerves increases.*

Loosen up Your Shoulders

Fran, 38, a sculptor who lives in New York City, supports herself by driving a taxi. She found that at first the tensions of her job were going straight into her shoulders. At the end of the day they were tight and tense. She also found that she unconsciously started to hunch them up and forward rather than carrying them the proper way—down and back. A friend suggested a variety of shoulder exercises to do while waiting in traffic (when she did not have a fare).

1. Raise your shoulders to your ears. Then release and relax them.
2. Raise one shoulder at a time, contracting it while you relax the other.

3. With both hands on the steering wheel, rotate your shoulders in small circular motions, first forward, then backward.

4. Pull them back, as if trying to make your shoulder blades meet. Hold for a few seconds, then release.

Benefits: *When you relieve tension in your shoulders, you make good posture easier and allow energy to flow freely to your head.*

NOTE: The "Thinker" immortalized in Rodin's famous statue, is actually giving himself a serious handicap because thinking—and everything else—is done more effectively when your shoulders are not hunched.

Dispel a Foul Mood

Howard, 48, a stockbroker, was driving home. The market was weak and the stock he had been confidently recommending was falling fast. To make matters worse, his mother-in-law was visiting. Just then, a collision up ahead brought traffic to a standstill. It occurred to him that he had a choice. He could sit there, tense and frustrated, thirsting for a martini, or he could try to change his mood. He:

- Took a deep breath and tightened every muscle in his body. As he exhaled, he relaxed his muscles and pictured all the tension leaving his body and mind.

- Pictured himself sitting on a mountain top, looking down at the distant traffic jam. He imagined a gentle rain pouring over and through him, washing away the stock market, his irritated customers, and the problems at home.

By the time the traffic started moving again, Howard could even see some good qualities in his mother-in-law!

When irritated and forced to wait, you may choose to re-experience a favorite pleasure or a former triumph—a fishing trip, a gourmet meal, or a winning poker hand. Vividly picture yourself participating in the scene. Be keenly aware of your environment. Involve as many of your senses as possible.

Benefits: *Your mood will brighten and your body will no longer suffer from the negative effects of irritation and stress. (The subconscious, which affects so many of our body responses, does not* differentiate—as does our conscious mind—between events taking place in our imagination or in the "real" world.)

NOTE: Any visualization exercise is more effective when preceded by body relaxation. (See "Relieve Anxiety and Tension," and "Programming Your Subconscious.")

Increase the Vitality of Your Face

Giselle, 52, a yoga teacher, beautifully represents what she teaches and practices. She is never sick, and you have to look hard to find a wrinkle. While driving, she does a modified version of the Lion Pose when stopped at an intersection.

1. Inhale deeply through nose.
2. Hold breath for a few seconds while sticking out tongue as far as possible (try to touch your chin). Open your eyes as wide as you can.
3. Exhale through an open mouth, making a "H-a-a" sound.

Benefits: *For many years, practitioners of yoga have claimed that the Lion Pose increases the vibrant appearance of the face by stimulating circulation. It is also reputed to help prevent or eliminate wrinkles around the eyes and to discourage colds, sore throats, and unwanted admirers.*

Tone and Beautify Your Arms

First Lady Michelle Obama, at an official government occasion, made fashion news by displaying her youthful, sexy arms in a sleeveless dress.

This inspired Bella, a slightly aging socialite, to look carefully at her own bare arms. They were neither sleek, nor smooth, nor sexy. She devised an emergency exercise:

- When being driven in her tinted-glass limo, she sometimes takes a full breath—then she lifts her arms over her head and pushes against the car ceiling, palms flat, exhaling slowly.

If you're not a celebrity afraid of scandal-sheet photographers, you can do this while stopped at a red light, or any time you are a passenger in a car.

Benefits: *This exercise reduces muscle flab and tones the arms. It also helps to create the habit of straightening the spine and feeling one's torso lifted from the waist.*

WAITING
In a Crisis

Mastering Emergencies

A small plane carrying five people had to crash land in a cold, mountainous region. All suffered minor injuries. They had no food, but the snow provided water. It took three days for a rescue team to reach them. Only one man managed to remain relaxed, cheerful, and free of frostbite. How did he do it?

He had once taken a self-hypnosis workshop to stop smoking. He applied the same principles to his current situation. They could be useful to anyone who is forced to wait during an emergency. This is what he did:

- He got himself into a deeply relaxed state and in touch with his subconscious mind. (See "Program Your Subconscious.")
- He imagined himself on a beautiful beach, basking in the sun and feeling healing energy warming his body and restoring it to health.
- He told himself, "As I lie here relaxing, time will pass quickly. Very soon I will be found."
- He kept his mind focused on a favorite line of poetry. He repeated it continuously and ignored all other thoughts and sensations.

Benefits: *Time can be made to pass quickly. Many of the traumatic aspects of an emergency can be minimized or avoided. It may even become in some ways a positive experience. This applies to virtually any emergency waiting situation whenever you're stuck in an elevator, a traffic jam, at the airport, etc.*

NOTE: The subconscious has played a part in two heroic survival stories. One man survived eight years of solitary confinement as a political prisoner by using a spot on the wall to put himself into a trance. And an American prisoner of war endured years of torture by continuously repeating a line from a philosopher he had read in school.

Harness Anger

Henrietta, 25, still had two children in diapers when twins arrived. After that, exhaustion was her normal condition. One day, just as her husband, his words slightly slurred, called to say he was bringing his boss home for dinner in one hour, Mark hit Jenny with a banana, Jenny then wrote her name with black magic marker on the new beige living room rug.

Henrietta's first impulse was to slap and scream, but she caught herself and waited to cool off. She remembered the saying, "If you blow up, you'll blow it." She visualized a snapshot of the scene—and saw herself laughing about it ten years later. While thawing a steak, she called her best friend and talked about her angry feelings. Then, when her husband arrived with his boss, she was feeling relaxed and quite cheerful. She was even able to joke about the artist's signature on the floor.

Some suggestions for waiting to cool off when you see red:

- Make yourself wait for a few moments, but don't repress your feelings. Then express them, but don't accuse the other person: talk only about how you yourself feel. This may be easier after discussing the situation with someone uninvolved.

- Imagine how the situation would look to you in ten years, immortalized in a snapshot. Humor heals.

- Avoid the refrigerator.

- Imagine yourself surrounded by the color blue—it has a deeply calming effect. Some people visualize a cloud of blue light, take a deep breath, and imagine that they are inhaling this blueness.

- Above all, distract yourself (rather than brood about what happened): go for a walk, bake a cake, read something amusing. You'll give yourself breathing space.

Benefits: *Calmness, greater objectivity, and effective handling of the anger-causing situation. The ability and opportunity to explain your feelings without accusations that trigger hostile defensiveness in others.*

Banish Panic

Edwin, 23, was shaking on the edge of the stage. He had been preparing for this moment for months. He was about to describe and explain one of his musical compositions to a large audience—and then

perform it on the piano. As he heard himself being introduced, his heart was beating violently, his head felt dizzy, and his knees were knocking against each other. He wanted to run away. Suddenly, he remembered the advice of his high-school drama teacher. In a few moments, he stepped out boldly, spoke clearly, and played well. This is the advice he followed:

- Tighten your buttocks and legs; then completely relax them. Concentrate on feeling the relaxation in your legs.

- Take a deep breath, and exhale slowly.

- If you have time, close your eyes for a moment and visualize a beautiful blue sky. This color is deeply relaxing.

Benefits: *A calmness and presence of mind help you to perform effectively. Simply knowing there is something you can do if you start to feel panicky is a help in itself—it banishes the fear of fear.*

NOTE: According to some recent surveys, fear of public speaking has replaced fear of death as the source of greatest anxiety. The exercises above are easy to do, take only a moment, and work.

Decrease Mugability

Bernie, 33, a newspaper reporter who regularly walked dangerous city streets, was puzzled. Many people he knew had been mugged, yet he had never been bothered. He felt perfectly safe. He became interested in the question, "Who is most likely to be mugged?" He came across a recent study in which convicted muggers were shown videotapes of pedestrians and rated them according to their "mugability." Surprisingly, the ones voted "most mugable" were not the most frail-looking, nor were they the oldest. Although the muggers could not explain why, they generally agreed about the most likely choices. Bernie saw a definite pattern.

The following characteristics make you attractive to muggers:

- Appearing easy to topple. Leaning too far forward. Rigid posture.
- A face that communicates mixed emotion. If the mouth looks determined but there is fear or suspicion in the eyes, a mugger senses a victim.
- Tense, hunched shoulders. They signal fear or insecurity.
- A lack of unified direction. If arms or head move sideways instead of in harmony with the body, the message is, "I don't know where I'm going."

Muggers will avoid you if you have the following:

- A firm, solid stance.
- A unified expression on your face. The eyes, mouth, and tilt of the head all combine to express the same purposeful feeling.
- Relaxed shoulders.
- A sense of direction communicated by the whole body.

All this seems to illustrate the "Law of Attraction," as discussed in the Abraham teachings, "The Secret," and other new-age advice books. A man who rented an apartment once observed: "Every time I had occasion to knock on the door of the woman who lived below me, I heard her unlock one lock after another from the top to the bottom of the door. She was intensely afraid of being mugged. And guess what? Time after time, when she went out, she got mugged. Evidently, her fearful vibes drew the muggers to her."

- Create a forceful presence, as if you "own the place."
- Anyone who has this last quality usually has the first four.

Some people seem to be able to evoke this quality unconsciously. With others, it is apparently a by-product of their sense of power or achievement. Let us examine two Eastern techniques for attaining this forceful presence: Centering and Grounding. These can be practiced anywhere you stand and wait.

Centering is a focusing upon an instinctually conscious center of gravity within your own body. When you have this awareness, you seem to be better balanced and harder to topple. Your "center" is about 2 to 4 inches below your navel and equidistant between the front of your body and your spine. Visualize it as a soft, warm ball suspended like a gyroscope. Karate and other Eastern systems of movement develop a consciousness of this center.

When you walk, feel yourself being pulled forward from this center. Your shoulders will tend to relax, and your body will give a more integrated and forceful impression.

Grounding is a strong sense of being directly supported by the earth. It is the feeling that you are almost a part of—or extend from—the ground beneath you.

- Concentrate on your feet and feel their relationship to what they stand on. Feel your relaxed weight on the earth, as if you could almost sink into it.
- Be sure that your knees are not locked.

- Take a deep breath. As you inhale, feel as if you are drawing energy from the earth into your own body. As you exhale, feel a solid connection between your body and the ground beneath you.

Benefits: *Muggers leave you alone. You will communicate a sense of solid strength and a more forceful presence. You will be able to draw more effectively on two invaluable sources: your inner strength and the earth.*

WAITING
For a TV Program to Resume

Four Commercials to Fitness

Marcie, 45, a single mother and a pathologist at a major research hospital, took a critical look at herself in the mirror. Much of her was getting too soft, spread out, even sagging. Her body seemed to be saying, "How about taking a little time for me?" But Marcie needed the spare time she had to unwind in front of the TV in the evening. Fortunately, she ran into an exercise expert who told her that forty minutes a week was all she needed to achieve minimal fitness.

  She realized his recommendations would equal the TV time for four commercials a night on four evenings a week. Here are the four short exercises she used.

- *First Break:* Limber up. Stand with your feet about two feet apart. Keep your abdominal muscles tight.

- Loosen up your shoulders by lifting, dropping, and rotating them forward and backward.

- Reach up as high as possible, one arm at a time.

- Keeping lower body stationary, twist upper body and head as far as possible in each direction.

- Do the Woodchopper: Swing the arms overhead; then swing

upper body and arms down to reach as far as possible between the legs.

Do the Sideways Slide (this is an excellent waist-trimmer):

1. Stand with legs comfortably apart, arms at your sides. Bend from side to side, sliding your hands along your sides as you do so. (When you bend to the right, your right hand slides down your right leg and your left hand moves up toward your left armpit.)

2. Make these sliding movements slowly; feel your sides stretch.

3. As you do this, don't bend forward. Keep your knees straight and abdomen flat.

Second Break: Wall Push-ups for upper-body toning.

1. Stand about three feet from a wall. Put hands straight ahead on wall, shoulder height.

2. Lean forward until your chest comes near the wall. (Keep body in a straight line.)

3. Push away until you return to starting position.

When you can do twenty easily in this position, make the exercise harder:

- Move further from the wall. When this gets too easy:

- Push against a stable piece of furniture which is closer to the ground.

- Eventually you will be doing these on the floor, at first keeping your knees on the floor, then keeping your body straight.

Third Break: Ease-backs for toning the abdomen.

1. Sit on the floor, knees bent, feet hooked under a piece of furniture.

2. Press chin to chest, round spine, and tighten abdominals (as if someone were pressing you in the stomach).

3. Put hands on abdomen so that you can feel the muscles tighten as you slowly lower your upper body away from your knees. Move only a few inches down at first, then return. Keep moving back a little at a time to the spot which requires some effort to hold for about 20 seconds. You are making it challenging enough for yourself if your abdominal muscles start to quiver during the last few seconds.

4. As the muscles get stronger, move ever closer to the floor.

Ease-backs ensure that your abdominal muscles do the work, whereas conventional sit-ups often rely on shoulder or back muscles.

Fourth Break: Aerobic Exercises for your cardio-vascular system. (This takes 5 minutes, so you may want to combine the commercial break at the end of a program with the short lead-in for the next one, plus its first commercial.)

1. Run in place, dance, or jog on a mini-trampoline for 5 minutes.

2. Start slowly and take the last minute to taper off, so that your body has a chance to warm up into vigorous exercise and to cool down.

3. After you stop, walk around a bit. Then sit back and enjoy your program. Cover yourself if you start to feel too cool.

Once you have established an aerobic routine you are comfortable with, you may wish to increase the efficiency of the exercise by adding hand weights. A small weight in each hand adds to upper-body conditioning, burns extra calories, and increases the benefits to the cardiopulmonary system.

- Start with no more than one pound in each hand. Cans of soup or beans will do. Eventually you may progress to two- or three-pound weights.

- The exercise becomes more efficient as you lift your hands higher and move more quickly.

- Eventually you may wish to add to the efficiency of the limbering up exercises (*see First Break*) by using light weights with some of them.

- Many physicians recommend that anyone over 35 undergo a stress test before starting a vigorous exercise program. Such a test determines the exact maximum heart rate for that individual, who then is directed to maintain a training rate of 60-80 percent of that maximum.

Benefits: *You look and feel better with minimal time and effort.*

Note: Exercise may become so enjoyable and may make you feel so good that you may eventually extend your aerobics to the 15-30 minute time span recommended by most exercise experts.

The mini-trampoline is especially addicting. The zero-gravity you experience for a fraction of a second during each step seems to be particularly refreshing and energizing. It is easy on your joints, stimulates

your lymph system, and massages every cell in your body. One-pound weights held in each hand and lifted at each step greatly add to the efficiency of the exercise. And you can watch TV while you do it.

Revitalize Your Spine

Florence, 73, retired school teacher, likes to do the Gentle Bend during commercial breaks.

1. While sitting in a chair, take a deep breath.
2. As you exhale, let your whole upper body curl slowly toward the floor, one vertebra at a time.
3. Come up slowly as you inhale.
4. Let your head and neck be the last to return to a normal sitting position.

Benefits: *Improves circulation, releases tension, keeps the spine flexible and brings a glow to the face. And you don't even have to get out of your chair!*

Tone Your Lower Body

Joe, 55, a plant manager, was having trouble reading his bathroom scale. A large beer belly was blocking the view. Another football season was about to start. As he groped for his beer in the refrigerator, preparing to settle down in front of the TV, he found only carrot sticks, ice water, and two magazine articles his wife had placed there. One praised the revitalizing effects of carrots on male potency and the other touted physical fitness. Among many bothersome exercises, Joe did find one that he could conveniently do during commercials—the Knee Lift.

1. Sit comfortably on chair or couch. Clasp hands behind neck.

2. Lift your right knee off the floor and touch it to your left elbow. Alternate legs.

3. Keep your lower spine pressed comfortably against the chair.

When you feel stronger, do the exercise with your legs off the floor. It's just like riding a bicycle.

Benefits: *A pleasant way to tone the mid-section and promote the health of the vital organs—especially for people unaccustomed to exercise.*

Diminish Fatigue and Wrinkles

Christine, 27, a housewife, mother, and physical therapist, likes to relax with television. During commercials and while waiting for her program to resume, she often does the Half Shoulder Stand, especially when she is very tired.

1. Lie down on the floor (a folded blanket or exercise mat is helpful). Place hands at sides, palms down. Keep your feet together.

2. Bend knees to your chest, then extend legs toward the ceiling.

3. Lift hips off the floor, supporting them with your hands. Keep your elbows close together on the floor.

4. Start by holding this position for only half a minute; work up to the entire commercial break.

5. Keep breathing comfortably the whole time.

6. To come down, bend both knees toward your face, place your palms flat on the floor and start to lower yourself, one vertebra at a time.

7. Hips come down first; then slowly lower the legs. Lie quietly and relax for a moment before you get up.

Benefits: *There is no better way to relieve fatigue or to give the face a healthy glow. No exercise is more effective against wrinkles. It relieves varicose veins and hemorrhoids and is known as a restorer of youth and vitality.*

Take a Stretch Break

Jerry and Sue, government employees in their late fifties, are surprisingly youthful and healthy. For them a commercial break is often a stretch break. Doing it together makes it fun.

- Stand with feet shoulder-width apart, arms reaching toward ceiling. Stretch first one arm up from the waist, then the other. Do several with each arm.

- Raise arms straight over your head. Stretch down toward one side, then the other. Do several sets slowly.

- Bend down loosely from the waist, keeping knees unlocked. Come up slowly, one vertebra at a time.

Benefits: *As the old yoga saying goes, "You are as young as your spine is flexible."*

Flatten Your Stomach

Harold, 48, a middle manager, lost his job. The beers he drank while watching more TV were showing up around his waist. And weak abdominal muscles were contributing to lower-back pain. He made an iron-clad rule to do sit-ups during the first commercial each evening.

The Curl-Up:

1. Lie on your back, knees lifted to chest, and ankles crossed.
2. Place hands behind head.

3. Slowly curl up head, neck, and shoulders. Touch elbows to knees. Then roll back down slowly.

Do the whole exercise slowly and with control.

- Beginners should aim at getting only the top part of the shoulders off the floor.
- Start with 10 repetitions and work up to 3 sets of 20.

While doing The Curl-Up, breathe out as you curl up; breathe in as you roll back down. (This applies to most other exercises: breathe out as you apply pressure and breathe in as you relax.)

Benefits: *A flatter stomach; also, stronger abdominal muscles and, thus, less chance of back trouble.*

The Curl-Up flattens faster than you can say, "Abolish those abominable abdominals."

WAITING

To Become Fully Awake

Stretch and Tone

Lilias, PBS yoga celebrity, believes that the way you spend the first few minutes makes a tremendous difference in the rest of your day.

Yoga wisdom teaches that to jump directly onto your feet from a deep sleep is a shock to the nervous system. Take a tip from nature: Stretch your way leisurely out of sleep, as dogs and cats do.

- Lying on your back, fully stretch first one side of your body, then the other, reaching as far as you can with each arm and leg. Yawn as you stretch.

- Flex and point your ankles and wrists and wiggle your toes.

- Slowly turn your head from side to side.

- Place the soles of your feet on the mattress and press the small of your back into the bed.

The following exercises may also be helpful:

For a smooth and young-looking neck—and a firm abdomen:

1. Place a folded pillow under your shoulders as you lie on your back. This allows your head to drop back.

2. Now lift your head high enough to see your heels, and lower it again. Inhale as you drop the head back; exhale as you bring it forward. (Start with five and work up to several sets of twenty.)

For waist and hips:

1. Lie on back, arms extended to sides of bed.

2. Slowly raise one leg toward the ceiling, then cross it over the body, bringing the foot as close as possible to the opposite hand.

3. Both knees are slightly bent. Shoulders remain on the bed, but hips are allowed to roll.

4. Bring the leg up again and lower it slowly.

Do several with each leg. (Sometimes doctors recommend this exercise for relief of tension or pain in the lower back.)

For circulation in feet and legs (these are ancient Oriental exercises):

▓ While lying on your back, rub the soles of your feet together.

▓ Rub the top and sides of each foot with the other foot, reaching up with each foot as high as is comfortable to rub the other leg.

For all the organs in the abdominal cavity (a traditional Chinese health-maintaining exercise):

1. With the palm of either hand, starting with the navel, rub your abdomen in increasingly larger circles.

2. Then change direction, rubbing in increasingly smaller circles.

The aim of this exercise is to build up some warmth in the abdominal cavity. It is important to keep your mind on this exercise as you do it.

(Ancient Chinese tradition holds that if you rub only in a clockwise direction—the direction in which it is believed the bowels move— you will help relieve constipation.)

Benefits: *You begin your day with energy and a sense of well-being. Without stiffness or sluggishness, it is easier to face life cheerfully.*

By devoting one minute in the morning to an exercise for a specific problem, you accomplish two important things:

1. Progress is made toward eliminating that particular problem.

2. You begin your day with a feeling of control over your life. The sense of mastery will become habitual and will carry over into the other areas of your day.

Program Your Day

Earnest, 31, a psychotherapist, suggests using the few seconds after awakening to Visualize Your Day The Way You Want It To Go. We are like computers, he believes: we need to make sure that the programming implanted in both our conscious and subconscious minds is working toward what we desire. The images that have been implanted in our subconscious during the course of our lives form a powerful undercurrent, a hidden map of attitudes and reactions. (There may be old resentments or memories of failure that could thwart our goals.)

During the moments we drift out of (or into) sleep, our subconscious is more readily available to us. These moments are particularly effective for creating and implanting the images of what we wish to be or to achieve.

- Picture yourself with correct posture, radiantly attractive, and in tune with the people around you.
- Visualize the challenges of the day successfully met, your goals attained.

Benefits: *As you perceive yourself—at all levels of your mind—so you will be perceived, and so you will become.*

Invigorate Instantly

Bailey, 43, dynamic TV anchor man, takes a shower every morning.
While waiting for the water to reach the right temperature, he does the
Flying Jackknife.

1. Clasp hands behind your back, arms toward the floor.

2. Inhale while pulling your shoulders back and chest up. Use the
   abdominal muscles to help support the lower back.

3. As you exhale, slowly bend forward, raising the arms overhead.

4. Try to get your head close to your knees. Raise arms as far over
   your head as possible. If this puts strain on your knees, bend
   them as you exhale.

Benefits: *Instant invigoration. This exercise also releases tension and stiffness in the neck and shoulders.*

Improve Your Circulation

Genevieve, 49, a highly efficient executive secretary, has started to develop circulation problems. Whenever possible, she takes off her shoes under her desk at work, wiggles her toes and rotates her ankles. While waiting for her shower to reach the correct temperature, she brushes her body with a natural-bristle brush.

Benefits: *The increased circulation makes your body feel more alive and vibrant. Some great beauties claim that gentle brushing of the face keeps their complexions glowing and wrinkle-free.*

WAITING
....
To Fall Asleep

Tight Float and Complete Breath

Carl, 55, recently promoted vice-president in charge of product development at a soap company, suffered from insomnia because of new pressures. Four martinis and a slab of rare roast beef before bed seemed to help until his doctor declared, "You're in deep trouble." Carl took up racquetball and lost ten pounds. Now, to fall asleep, he practices the Tight Float.

1. Tense every muscle in your body, including your face, while holding your breath for a moment.

2. Exhale as you relax and sink into the mattress.

Picture yourself floating on a cloud or on a raft in a calm and beautiful lake. Be aware of your breathing. Slowly lengthen the time for each full breath. For many people, the Complete Breath will induce deep relaxation:

1. With your mouth closed, breathe deeply through your nose. Exhale.

2. As you take your next breath, fill your abdomen with air, ballooning it slightly.

3. Fill your lungs with air.

4. Exhale, releasing air slowly from your lungs and abdomen, imagining that you are deflating a balloon.

Benefits: *You slip into sleep easily and pleasantly. Deep, slow breathing is good for body and mind in almost any situation.*

Lazy Buddha

Harold, 47 and on the corporate fast track, finds the Lazy Buddha very relaxing as he waits to fall asleep.

1. Sit cross-legged on your bed.

2. Lie back, keeping your legs crossed on the bed.

3. Hold for a while . . .

4. Then stretch out and relax.

Benefits: *Relaxes your lower back. You naturally breathe deeply in this position. The more tension you get rid of before you fall asleep, the deeper and more restful your sleep.*

Breaking Your Belt

Bill, 39, head of his own company and member of the Young
President's Club, advises Breaking Your Belt as the simplest method of
falling asleep:

- Balloon out your abdominal muscles as if trying to break your
  belt. (As you do so, breathe in slightly but not deeply.)

- Hold as long as you can, while breathing normally. Then relax.

Bill has never heard of anyone doing more than twenty before falling
asleep. Usually 4 or 5 will do it, even for hyperactive children.

Benefits: *Falling asleep sooner; a more relaxed sleep; firmer
abdominal muscles.*

Weight-Reducing Visualization

Frank, 51, a corporate lawyer, saw his waistline becoming a victim of
the tax-deductible lunch. He took a weight-reduction workshop and
learned a Visualization Exercise to do while waiting to fall asleep.

- Picture extra alcohol, butter, bread, and pastries turning to lard.

- Visualize yourself choosing moderate amounts of lean meat or
  fish, succulent salads, and vitamin-packed vegetables.

- See yourself as lean and full of energy, even if still slightly hungry. (The word "sad," experts tell us, derived originally from the word "sated.")

Benefits: *Fattening foods will no longer appeal to you, and you will be satisfied with just the amount of food your body needs.*

"A moment on the lips, a long time on the hips."

Putting Your Subconscious to Work

Arabella, 45, a novelist, has suddenly broken through a case of writer's block. Her new secret: while waiting to fall asleep at night, she poses the next day's writing problem to her subconscious. After she has delegated this responsibility, she falls asleep quickly and happily. The trick is in the trust—she expects to have the problem solved in the morning. And it usually is.

This is a more deliberate and precise version of the centuries-old practice of "sleeping on it" and making a decision in the morning. The more serious and complicated the problem, Arabella finds, the more imperative it is to let your subconscious work on it during the night. After all, your subconscious does not sleep—and accepts fewer limitations than your conscious mind. Pose the problem to it clearly— and expect a meaningful answer when you awaken.

Benefits: *An effective solution to a problem—without losing sleep or tiring your conscious mind.*

The Stomach Flattener

Wallace, 58, a manufacturing-company president, kept waking up at two or three a.m. He would lie in bed for hours, wide awake. Finally he decided to use that time to get rid of his developing paunch. Within two weeks the change was noticeable, and now, ten years later, he is the only man among his friends without a protruding pot. Most important for him, the exercise he discovered gets him relaxed and tired enough to sleep soundly for the rest of the night.

This is what he does:

1. Lying in bed, under the covers, place your hands, palms down, under your buttocks. (This reduces the strain on your back.)
2. Bend your legs and place feet flat on the bed.
3. While tightening your abdominal muscles, lift your feet so that they are barely off the bed.

4. Let them drop.

You may wish to start with only five or ten repetitions. As your abdominal muscles get stronger, you can hold your raised legs for a few seconds before you let them drop.

Wallace worked up to 100 repetitions, 20 slow ones and the rest quickies.

Benefits: *A flat stomach and relaxed, sound sleep.*

WAITING

In Almost Any Situation

BODY BASICS

Lorraine, 37, a sales lady in an elegant clothing salon, spends much of her day standing and waiting for the customer with a beautiful new dress in her eyes. The following unobtrusive exercises help keep Lorraine cheerfully alert and energetic.

- Picture a cardboard Halloween skeleton hung by the top of its head. Imagine your head being pulled up as if there were a string attached to the top of it. Let the rest of your body hang loosely.

The shoulders hang down and the upper body is pulled from the waist. There is an open feeling in your chest and pelvis. Visualize your tailbone hanging loosely toward the floor.

- Keep your weight on both feet, knees slightly bent. Allow your body to sway or move when it wishes. (A rigid position can cause tension and fatigue.)

- It may help lower-back pain to prop one foot up on a stool or step if standing for an extended period.

- Stand with your back against a wall, knees slightly bent. Press your abdomen toward your spine as if someone pushed you in the stomach, and press your spine into the wall. Hold for a few seconds, then release.

- Wear clothes that make you feel attractive. You are much less likely to slump and cramp your internal organs if you know that you look great. (How's that for a good excuse for new clothes?)

Benefits: *You look better, feel better, and have more energy.*

The Best Way to Sit

Adele, 36, is a beauty and fitness teacher who gives demonstrations and workshops all over the country. She spends a lot of time sitting and waiting at airports, in restaurants, and backstage in television studios. She recommends that every chair be used as a posture and exercise aid:

- With your back leaning against the chair, keep your shoulders loose and relaxed and your spine long. Try not to slump. Your

weight should be evenly on both hips. It is good to have a feeling that your upper body is being pulled up from the waist—not just your shoulders, but your whole upper body.

- Move around and shift positions frequently. If you've been sitting close to an hour, get up and walk around.

- Sitting as described above, breathe slowly into your abdomen, ballooning it out as you inhale. As you exhale, slowly deflate the abdomen and press your lower back into the chair.

- Clasp your hands behind your back. Keeping your arms straight, squeeze your shoulder blades together, trying to touch your elbows together.

Benefits: *Improves posture, releases tension in your shoulders, helps to strengthen your abdominal muscles, and keeps you feeling relaxed and alert.*

What Every Woman Should Do

Eloise, a sex therapist in her late thirties, urges all her female patients to do contracting exercises to tone the vaginal muscles. She believes that all women can benefit from these exercises.

- *The Kegel Exercise:* This exercise consists of rhythmically contracting the muscles of the pelvic floor, as if to stop urinating. Hold this position tightly for a moment; then relax. Do several sets of 10. Many doctors and sex therapists recommend at least 100 a day.

- This can be done while standing, sitting or lying anywhere.

Although a doctor is credited with developing this exercise, it has been an important part of Taoist health practices for 6000 years and has been used widely by Asian women.

Benefits: *It maintains and restores the elasticity and tone of the muscles of the vagina. It is reputed to contribute significantly to a woman's pleasure and skill in lovemaking. It has also been recommended by doctors for urine-leakage problems and for restoring vaginal tone after childbirth. This exercise is recommended for all women in order to improve the pelvic support system. As women get older, the need for this exercise increases.*

NOTE: ALSO FOR MEN: Doctors frequently prescribe Kegels for men, to strengthen the PC (pubococcygeus muscle)—for prostate pain, for urinary incontinence, for stronger orgasms, and for premature ejaculations. These invisible exercises can be done any time, and can keep boring meetings from being a complete waste of time.

Invisible Posture Exercise

Myra, 16, grew too tall too fast. Posture was a problem. Her gym teacher suggested an exercise that can be done in almost any waiting moment.

1. Clasp your hands behind your back.
2. Try to bring your elbows as close together as possible.
3. Don't let your stomach stick out or your back sway.

Benefits: *Chest gets pulled up, shoulders go back and down, and spine straightens. This can be done while sitting, standing, or walking.*

A Move to Better Posture

Sophia has taught body awareness and movement for thirty years. She believes that the principles of good posture are not generally understood.

When your posture is poor, your muscles are doing work that should be done by your bones. It should be the work of the bones to support your weight against the pull of gravity. If muscles do this job, energy is wasted. Also, your muscles are prevented from fulfilling their main function, which is to provide easy and efficient movement.

The best posture is that which allows you to move as easily and efficiently as possible in all directions. Sophia advocates an exercise that allows you to feel how this principle functions. She calls it The Invisible Pencil.

- Pretend there is a long pencil growing straight up from the floor through the middle of your body and out the top of your head. Imagine that the pencil is drawing small circles on the ceiling. But here is the key: this subtle circular movement starts from your ankles.

- Do a few circles first in one direction, then the other. Feel the weight of your body as it is carried by your skeleton. Let it sink into the floor.

- This movement should be so small that no one will notice, even in a crowded elevator or theater line.

- As you finish this exercise, try to maintain the feeling of being physically centered and supported by the ground.

Benefits: *You feel in your own body a key ingredient of good posture, and it becomes much easier to improve yours. As your muscles are freed from the work of carrying your body weight, you experience greater energy and move more easily and efficiently.*

Standing Isometrics

Jason, 27, is working his way through law school as a messenger. His life is hectic and he has no time for exercise. Much of his working time is spent standing and waiting. To keep himself in shape, he does Standing Isometric Exercises. Hold each position for a few seconds:

- Forcefully pull in your abdomen, as if you wanted it to touch your backbone.

- Press your inner thighs together, as if there were a magnet between your legs.

SAMSON

▓ Clasp your hands in front of your chest; press them together. Then try to pull them apart.

▓ Fold your arms in front of your chest with your palms resting just above your elbows. Push.

▓ Push your palms against the insides of a doorway—first with palms at shoulder height, then at hip level.

▓ Fold your arms behind you, your palms gripping your forearms. Push your arms together; then try to pull them apart.

Benefits: *You can greatly improve the shape and tone of your body with a minimum of time and no special equipment. Maximum benefits are obtained when each pose is held for 6 to 10 seconds.*

NOTE: Isometric and other static exercises should not be done by anyone with high blood pressure or certain heart conditions. If in doubt, consult a physician.

It's in Your Hands

Charlotte, 44, a medical doctor, does not take two aspirin when she gets a tension headache. If she feels the start of a sore throat or a touch of indigestion after gulping down a meal, she does not reach for a pill.

She has discovered Reflexology, the Western version of the ancient Chinese science of acupuncture. Both are based on the premise that the body contains a network of nerves on which energy travels. Reflexology involves no needles, only firm pressure with fingers on either hands or feet. The pressure is deep enough to feel bone or muscle.

Charlotte does this hand massage anywhere, anytime she needs it and her hands are free. Almost any waiting moment can be used.

- *For headaches:* pressing along thumbs will eliminate most. Keep pressing along thumb; if you find a sore spot, massage it for a few minutes, then move on. Some headaches require pressure on the first finger and on the web between thumb and first finger. (It works for hangovers too!)

- *For sore throats or tension along back of neck:* Press along bottom of thumb and along the corner of the thumbnail which is closest to the index finger.

- *For stomach problems:* press area between thumb and first finger. Some people habitually massage this area after every meal, to promote optimum digestion.

- *If you feel cold:* massage your third and fourth fingers. (Acupuncturists believe that the fourth finger particularly contains the reflex for the mechanism which controls the temperature of the body.)

Benefits: *The keys to our health and well-being are to some extent literally in our hands. (For any serious medical problem, check with your doctor.)*

The Slimming Image

Ellie May, 47, is founder and manager of the famous Slendertime Weight Reduction Centers. Among her clients are busy professional people who don't take time for regular physical exercise. She advises them to use their waiting time for calorie-burning and body-toning activities:

- Keep in motion whenever possible. Walk while waiting for the elevator or subway. Shift your weight from one foot to the other while standing in line.

- Alternately tighten and release abdominal, seat or other muscles when appropriate and convenient. (See "Standing Isometric Exercises")

The major secret of Ellie May's success is her emphasis on a positive self-image. She believes that we must discard all negative feelings—both about ourselves and about others. In her opinion, these feelings contribute to overweight and ill health.

Any waiting moment can be used for focusing on the image of our best possible self. She warns against comparing or competing: you don't have to look like a particular model or movie star. Every man, every woman, she insists, can be himself or herself better than anyone else can.

Each of us has a unique strength and beauty—and an individual contribution to make. That which is good in us, she maintains, is our true reality. If our faults are not given the energy of our attention, they are more likely to fall away.

- Our extra pounds of fat fall away as we bring out the slim person within.

- The wrinkles around our eyes are less noticeable—and almost seem to fade away—when there is light and sparkle in our eyes.

- Our problems with the people around us fade away as we focus on the good that is in them.

- Ellie May glows with enthusiasm when she inspires her clients thus: "Let us see in our mind and in our consciousness the picture of our perfect self, and then step into the picture."

Benefits: *A positive self-image is invaluable for achieving the figure which is perfect for us.*

LOOK AND SEE BETTER

Invisible Face Exercise

Romero, 60, a professional poker player, is noted for his look of inscrutable concentration. Those playing against him don't realize that while waiting between bets, he is doing the Invisible Facial Isometric Exercises that contribute substantially to his youthful appearance.

- Dilate the nostrils. Flare them out.

- Concentrate on the muscle right above your forehead and under your hairline. Contract this muscle, pulling it back, smoothing the wrinkles on your forehead.

- Contract the fanlike muscle at each temple, between your eye and the upper edge of your ear. These are the muscles that support the sides of your face. When firm and strong, they give you youthful facial tone and firm-textured skin. As you learn to pull them back and up, you are actually giving yourself a facelift.

- It helps to raise the outside edge of your eyebrows and to think of pulling them back toward your ears. Then try to wiggle your ears.

A simpler version of this exercise:

- Think of your face as a sunflower in the process of opening. Your nose is the center. Feel the petals pulling back. Concentrate on the forehead and the sides of your face.

Benefits: *You look younger. Many famous people have done this exercise. No one can tell that you are exercising!*

Yawning as a Facial Exercise

Josephine, 53, wife of a prominent political advisor, noticed that men's faces seem to stay firmer as they age. Is it from tightening their faces as they shave? She learned to turn every yawn, discreetly covered by her hand, into a surprisingly beneficial exercise.

If you yawn while you wait, don't yawn in vain:

- Cover your open mouth with your hand. Curl lips over teeth.
- As you close your mouth slowly, tense the corners of your mouth into a smile.
- Exaggerate each mouth position so that you feel the stretch in the muscles of your neck.

Benefits: *Tones and firms mouth area and cheeks. Also fights wrinkles and sagging muscles around the eyes and neck.*

NOTE: In gyms and health clubs, you often see men and women with smooth, firm bodies—and wrinkled, sagging faces. Workouts keep their bodies toned, but facial exercises could make them look much younger.

Eliminate Scowl Lines

Margaret, 58, successful real-estate agent, had developed some vertical lines between her eyebrows that made her seem to scowl. While waiting for clients to show up, she found several things she could do to diminish these lines.

- Using the muscles in your forehead, pull your eyebrows toward each other and down. (You are actually practicing frowning, but only in order to control the muscles involved.)
- Then pull eyebrows as far apart and up as possible.

For additional benefits:

1. Close eyes tightly while eyebrows are being pulled apart and up. (Tones and improves circulation of eye area.)

2. Press two fingers against scowl lines when practicing frowning. (Many facial exercises are more effective when done against resistance.)

3. Massage the frown lines firmly in all directions with the same two fingers.

   You should press firmly enough to feel the bone beneath the skin and muscle, but do not dig the nails into the skin.

Benefits: *A more pleasant and relaxed expression; a more youthful appearance.*

Refresh and Strengthen Your Eyes

Stephanie, 35, a researcher for a large law firm, found that pouring over precedents caused an increasing amount of eyestrain. Each day, both her eyes and her mind seemed to get tired more easily.

She took a weekend workshop in the principles of Do-in, a 10,000-year-old system of exercises that comes to us from the Far East by way of Japan. The eye exercises she learned, along with suggestions from a lawyer who had studied yoga, helped her immediately. She now takes several small "eye breaks" throughout her day.

The following exercises can be practiced during various waiting moments. They can be done separately or in combination.

- While sitting at a table or desk, close your eyes tightly for several seconds.

- As you relax your closed eyelids, rest your elbows on the table and cover both eyes completely with the palms of your hands. Put no pressure on the eyes. Feel the relaxation of total darkness.

- Take a few deep breaths, feeling your abdomen and ribs expand.

- As you exhale, imagine that the energy vibrations from your breath go to your eye area.

- With your eyes thus closed and covered, imagine that you are looking far into the distance—at endless green fields and blue skies.

- With eyes closed and covered, imagine in detail a scene which is at the same time pleasant, relaxing and full of motion. For example, visualize a beach scene. Observe the waves as they break, rush in, and recede, leaving the sand a darker color. Follow with your eyes a bright red beach ball as it is tossed by some youngsters.

This ancient practice of palming is the single most relaxing thing you can do for your eyes.

The following exercises use the pressure of the fingers to stimulate the circulation and the nerves of the eye area.

- Using the three middle fingers of either hand, press firmly along the bony ridges above and below the eyes. Move from the inner to the outer edge of the eye. You will discover points which are particularly sensitive; firm pressure on them is especially beneficial.

- Pinch the bridge of the nose and the corner of the eyes between your index finger and your thumb. Push upward firmly for a few seconds; then release suddenly.

Benefits: *The eyes are rested, refreshed, and strengthened. Also,* *people have noticed three additional benefits: the mind functions more effectively, eye disorders are alleviated, and wrinkles are diminished.*

NOTE: For additional benefit, splash cold water on your eyes at least twice a day.

Diminish Eye Strain and Frown Lines

Ethel teaches a course called "The Art of Seeing." Many of her suggestions fit almost any waiting situation:

- Blink often. This lubricates, cleanses, and rests your eyes. After reading for an hour, blink ten times: a "blink break" refreshes.

- Keep changing your focus. The eyes love motion and are strained by staring. Look into the distance, perhaps out a window, at moving objects—a bird, a swaying branch, a passing car or plane.

- Focus precisely on what you see. For example, when looking at a person's face, don't glance vaguely: shift your attention from one detail to another.

- Ask yourself several times a day: Is there tension in the eye area? Let it go. Relax your eyelids. Soften all the muscles in the eye area. Try to feel that your eyes are sinking into your head.

If convenient, practice "palming" (see previous section).

Avoid two energy-blocking faults:

1. Do not let your breathing become shallow and irregular when

something absorbs your total attention.

2. Do not let poor posture block the vital flow of blood and energy to your head.

Ethel recommends that while standing in line, you plant the lower half of your body firmly on the ground (see "grounding") and do The Triple Pull:

1. Feel yourself being pulled up from your breast bone.

2. Also feel the back top of your head being pulled straight up. This stretches the back of the neck and keeps the chin tucked in.

3. Pull your shoulders down and away from the ears. Keep your ears directly over your shoulders.

Benefits: *Eye strain is greatly diminished. Energy is increased. Posture is improved. Many of Ethel's students report better eyesight, plus elimination of frown lines and tension furrows. They look and feel more attractive and relaxed.*

Invisible Neck Exercise

Ellen, a high-powered stock-broker, has assembled a closet-full of turtleneck sweaters and blouses—to cover up and distract from her double chin and scrawny neck. She recently came across Cynthia Rowland's "invisible neck exercise." These are the directions she follows:

1. Lift your chin to create a taut line between your chin and the base of your neck. Keep your shoulders erect.

2. Press the surface of your tongue firmly against the roof of your mouth. Your teeth and lips will be slightly apart. Hold this contraction for a count of five.

3. Relax. Bring your head to its level position. Take a deep cleansing breath.

4. Do this exercise three times, ten seconds each.

Benefits: *A smooth and youthful neck. And if you have one, a vanishing double chin.*

Cynthia Rowland has devised a system of exercises for the face and neck which, if performed regularly, can reverse much of the sagging and wrinkling that are the side-effects of aging. You can look much younger without injections or surgery! Her system is appropriately called FACIAL MAGIC.

RELAXING AND ENERGIZING

Yawning to the Rescue

For Bert, 57, important contacts often lead to lucrative contracts. He runs his own consulting firm, and the pressure and stress levels of his work often contribute to tension headaches. Once, during a medical examination, Bert's physician caught him stifling a yawn. "Don't do that!" he said. "Your body is trying to release tension and heal itself." Thereupon followed a fascinating discourse on the importance and benefits of yawning. Here are its main points:

We yawn when we are bored. Boredom causes our breathing to become increasingly shallow. A yawn then serves to restore deeper and

more efficient breathing.

We also yawn when we are tired—when we need extra oxygen. Yawning produces a large, sudden intake of air to satisfy this need. And as the extra oxygen flows through the body, it helps to relax muscles and release tension.

During waiting moments we can make ourselves yawn using a technique suggested by Matthew Manning:

- With your mouth closed, sniff lightly through your nose several times.
- Then, with your mouth open, again sniff lightly through your nose several times.
- Very soon after this you will feel the urge to yawn.

How to get the most out of your yawn:

- Cooperate with it and relax into it.

- Hold your head high (but not tilted back) and let your mouth open wide.

- Let the yawn complete itself naturally. (Do not stifle it or cut it off.)

Benefits: *Yawning is an efficient way for the body to replenish its store of oxygen. It is also a valuable tension and stress release. The ability to yawn efficiently—and at will—is a useful tool for waiting moments.*

NOTE: Boredom produces tiredness and tension—hence, the expression "bored stiff." Yawning, a natural defense mechanism that provides more oxygen, can therefore be a reminder to take some full, deep breaths.

Stress Discovered and Dissolved

"But I *am* relaxed," declared Dr. Terra's client, annoyed with himself for being in a woman hypnotist's office. His mind kept wandering between yesterday's unpleasant board meeting and his wife's relatives who wanted a loan. He had not allowed himself to become aware of the ache in his neck and the tension headache that was gathering momentum.

"At least 60 percent of all illness can be related to psychosomatic factors," Dr. Terra observed. "If you feel a cold or other illness coming on, ask yourself if there is something you are avoiding facing, expressing, or doing." Her client gulped and stared. "Many problems can be solved by accepting responsibility for your own health and well-being. Tension blocks the body's energy, and the sooner you detect tension and apply a remedy, the better. First, try to get in touch with your body; try to become aware of the tensions, stresses, and discomforts it is feeling. Then you can do some specific exercises to nip trouble in the bud."

Many waiting moments can be used to scan your body for tension and discomfort:

- As you sit in a chair, focus on how your body feels. Are you allowing the back of the chair to give some support to your lower back? Is your body being held erect by your spine? (Remember that slumping is not relaxing. It puts undue pressure on the spine and tires it.)

- After you have adjusted your body to make yourself as comfortable as possible, scan it for tension. It helps to picture it as a field of light, with the areas of tension as dark spots in it.

- If there are some dark areas in your shoulders, lift each shoulder slightly, and consciously relax it as you let it drop. Feel its own weight pulling it down.

- If there are some tensions in your hands, shake them out gently, let them hang down a moment, feel their weight, and sense them relaxing. Then let them lie comfortably in your lap.

- To relax your legs, lift one at a time slightly, just long enough to feel its weight, then let it drop. Feel this weight being supported by the floor.

If you still feel any tension or discomfort in your body, do The Golden Laser:

- Visualize a cloud of golden light all around you. As you inhale, bring some of this light into your abdomen. Hold for several seconds; then, as you exhale slowly, imagine this light being beamed to the area of tension or discomfort. Visualize the darkness being dissolved. (Ancient Eastern wisdom teaches that breath heals and energizes.)

Benefits: *Stress-related troubles are discovered and dissolved early. You quickly regain vitality and a sense of well-being.*

NOTE: There is tremendous power in your mind and in the images it uses. Images are always floating through it—choose those that can contribute to your own radiant health and joyous vitality.

Pressing Stress Away

Janina, 70, is famous for her magic hands. Her children, grandchildren, and friends come to her with their tensions, aches, and complaints. A little rub and a few moments of pressing just the right place, and usually all is well. Once one of her grandsons was nervous about having to give a speech in front of the whole school. He developed an excruciating headache. She had him lie down and then worked on his head, shoulders, hands, and feet. To his great surprise, his headache was soon gone.

Janina suggests that during waiting moments we ourselves can do much to erase the effects of stress on our bodies.

- A healthy natural instinct makes people put the palms of their hands on their forehead. Tension is relieved by this method, and important nerves are stimulated.

- Tension often accumulates at the base of the skull, at the top of the spinal column. It helps to massage that area and put vibrating pressure on it with your fingertips.

- Press with fingertips along the top of the forehead, along the hairline.

- Massage the temples with a gentle rotating movement.

- Massage the top of the shoulders. Most people store tensions there. Press for a few seconds on any tender spots. Find the small indentation in the middle and press it with a vibrating movement. (This works even if you only have a minute and are fully clothed.)

- Grasp the large shoulder muscle next to the neck with the opposite hand. While holding it firmly, rotate the shoulder. Work on both shoulders this way.

- To relieve headaches, massage your fingers and toes. (Privacy is helpful when you work on your feet. See also the reflexology cure for headaches.)

- If you find any tender spot in the process of massaging, you get more effective relief if you can press down for 5 to 7 seconds.

Benefits: *When under stress, we put knots into ourselves that block our energy and mar our appearance. These knots can lead to pain or other problems. By dissolving them, we let our energy flow freely again.*

Relief from Tension

Chase, 64, has built a real-estate empire with a small investment and forty years of 16-hour days. Sacrificed along the way were four wives, three children, his nervous system, and his blood pressure. The only way he could relax was to pour down half a bottle of Scotch. When his fifth wife threatened to leave him, his physician suggested biofeedback therapy. Chase was directed to relax all parts of his body: his toes, the soles of his feet, his ankles, and so on. A machine monitored his brain waves and registered the degree of relaxation.

Chase was also given Visualization Exercises for relieving tension and stress. He found them especially effective before sleep but also used them successfully during other waiting moments. It is best to do them after relaxing your body as much as possible.

- Picture yourself walking along a wide field, holding a large bunch of helium balloons. Each balloon has written on it a particular problem or worry. Whatever thought comes to mind gets immediately imprinted on a balloon. After you've observed yourself walking along for a while, let the balloons go. Watch them float away.

- See your various worries and preoccupations written on a blackboard. Erase them.

- Picture yourself in your favorite place of relaxation. Bring in as many of your five senses as possible. If, for example, you see yourself by a brook in the woods, feel the coolness of the ground beneath you, the moist air against your face. Hear the rippling of the water, the gentle play of the wind in the tree branches.

Benefits: *Relief from stress and its negative physical effects. A greater sense of peace and well-being.*

Revitalization Exercise

Miriam, 39, the youngest and only female partner in a manufacturing firm, juggles the roles of wife, mother, and businesswoman. She rushes to make meetings on time, but it takes the men a while to arrive, get settled, and discuss yesterday's game. While waiting for the meeting to begin, she does the Revitalization Exercise.

1. Sit or stand in a comfortable position and straighten your spine.
2. Picture a ball of radiant energy above your head. Imagine that as you breathe deeply, you pull in this energy.
3. Hold this radiant energy in your body as you slowly exhale, visualizing all the tensions leaving your body and mind.

Benefits: *You are much more relaxed and pleasant after you've let go of past stresses and pains. There is no better cosmetic than vibrant energy.*

NOTE: Most people breathe 20 to 22 times per minute. Reducing this rate will increase your energy. Some advanced yogis breathe only 4 to 7 times per minute.

MIND STRATEGIES

Achieving Self-Confidence

Pamela, 37, assistant to a division head in a manufacturing firm, had been passed over for promotion. Moreover, the man in her life seemed only halfhearted in his attentions. And her mother was always criticizing her apartment, her appearance, and her single status. Then Pamela came across a survey of the qualities men admire most in women. Over 90 percent mentioned self-confidence. It was listed more frequently than any other quality, including physical beauty, sensitivity, femininity, or intelligence. She realized that she had been afraid to assert herself or show self-confidence out of fear of appearing unfeminine and frightening men away.

Pamela went to a personal-development workshop where she learned methods for coping with the negative things in her life and achieving a sense of her own worth. These methods can be used during almost any waiting moment.

- Clearly visualize a garbage bag. Put into it any negative thought or feeling that comes your way: every nasty remark, every feeling of failure or inadequacy. During waiting moments you can vividly imagine emptying the bag at a garbage dump—or dropping it from a cliff. Ecology-conscious people may prefer imagining themselves fertilizing a garden with it.

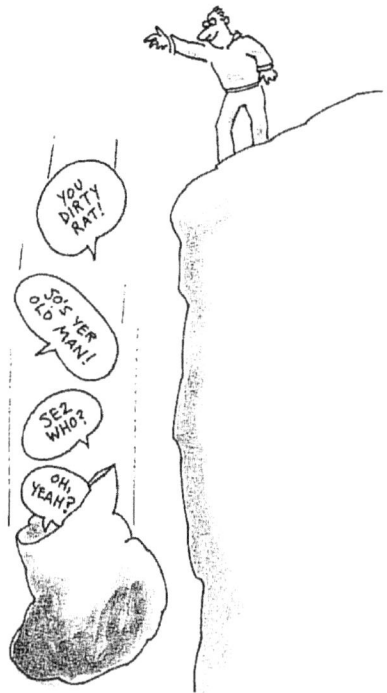

- Recall and re-experience moments that made you feel successful and worthy of respect and love. You can establish your own body signals for triggering these memories. For example:

- Touching thumb to forefinger recalls some of the nicest compliments you ever received.

- Straightening your posture brings back moments of great success.

- Clasping your hands evokes moments you have felt especially loved.

Benefits: *Having a system for disposing of negative thoughts, feelings, and experiences helps keep you from getting emotionally involved with them. It helps keep them out of the subconscious, where they can breed all sorts of mischief (anything from overeating to sabotaging relationships and even illness). By re-experiencing success, you create an invisible emotional armor that renders negative influences harmless. Positive images reprogram your subconscious for success and self-confidence.*

Self-confidence is the golden key to life's treasure house.

"Changing" Other People

In the beginning, Grace's cooking was a disaster area in her marriage to Jeff. He withheld comment—waiting until he could find something nice to say. One day she arranged the wieners gracefully with parsley on a platter. He praised, she beamed, and the next night she presented him with a dinner that was not only attractive but even delicious. Praise led to ever-greater success, and now Grace runs a catering service.

Many waiting moments can be used for planning to change someone.
This technique comes from the Ancient East:

- See the person vividly in your mind.

- Try to think of something good about the person.

- Try to evoke within yourself as much love (or at least positive feeling) for that person as you can.

- Breathe deeply into your chest area. In the middle of your chest, according to Eastern teachings, is your "heart center." As you breathe in, think of this center as expanding. Try to feel it opening, as if doors were swinging wide. A loving thought contributes to the feeling of opening.

- Practice getting in touch with this center when you see a tiny baby or someone you love. Try to feel the contrast between this expanding feeling and the sensation of closing in your chest when you see someone nasty who means you harm.

Benefits: *Unlike criticism, which can cause others to cling to (and defend) their undesirable qualities and habits, loving acceptance gives them the freedom and confidence to change. As you practice the above techniques, your positive feelings and thoughts will tend to affect your encounters with the person to be "improved." Ironically, changing the other person begins with you.*

Programming Your Subconscious For What You Desire

Ron, 42, sells industrial real estate. He already has the best sales record in the firm, although he is new at the job. Ron had started out in men's underwear in the basement of a department store. He was soon out-selling everyone else and was promoted to a department with more expensive merchandise. His present boss bought a TV from Ron and offered him a job on the spot.

Ron's air of self-confidence and his aura of success somehow glorify the product he sells. How does he do it?

We all know that "Nothing succeeds like success," but where do you start? You start where your personal records are kept—your subconscious mind.

Ron uses various waiting moments to program his subconscious mind for success. How does he reach his subconscious? Through Deep Relaxation and The Power of the Image. Here is how it can be done:

Deep Relaxation of body and mind. Use one or more of the following methods, depending on the situation and the time available to you:

- Slow down your breathing and make it deeper. Balloon out your abdomen as you inhale. Exhale twice as slowly as you inhale. Keep your mind on your breathing. (Body and mind automatically relax as you do this.)

- Progressively relax your body, starting with the feet. Some find it helpful to tense each body part, then relax it. Others find it sufficient to send suggestions to their toes, soles, ankles, etc., to relax. ("I concentrate on my toes; my toes are relaxed . . .")

- Pick a spot in front of you; keep looking at it as you blink your eyes 12 times. After you finally close your eyelids, they will feel very relaxed and tired. They will not want to open. (The relaxed sensation in the eyelids will automatically spread to the rest of your body.)

- Keeping your eyes closed, roll them up toward your eyebrows. (Putting your eyeballs in this position in a relaxed manner tends automatically to let you bypass the conscious mind and reach deeper levels.)

- As you take slow, deep breaths, see yourself exhaling tension and stress. Inhale peace.

- Choose a word you will keep repeating in order to reach a deeper level of your mind. As you breathe easily and naturally, repeat the word with each exhalation. Many people have had great success with the simple word "one." It has the advantage of having no distracting connotations. Others prefer a word with positive associations—peace, love, or light. Allow distracting thoughts to drift by, always returning to your word. Do this for several minutes—if you can, 5 minutes twice a day. It's important to maintain a passive attitude and just let the relaxation happen.

The Power of the Image. Deep relaxation gives you access to your subconscious; the image is the tool by which you can make it serve your purposes.

The following five steps have been found helpful for using deeper levels of the mind:

1. Count down from 10 to 1, telling yourself that at each descending number you are reaching a deeper level of your mind.

2. Visualize yourself floating downward to your favorite place of relaxation. This should be a place you have found especially relaxing at some pleasant moment in the past. See yourself there and re-experience the sensations of deep relaxation you once had. If you are tired, lingering

10 – DAFFY DUCK
9 – DONALD DUCK
8 – THE 3 STOOGES
7 – MICKEY MOUSE
6 – MR. ED
5 – LASSIE
4 – FLIPPER
3 – BEAVER CLEAVER
2 – MIKE HAMMER
1 – ALBERT EINSTEIN

here a few moments will refresh you as much as a long nap.

3. Now visualize a large stage in front of you. See it as a place of power. On it you imagine your world as you want it.

4. Your ideal self is on that stage: healthy, attractive, slim, self-confident and successful.

5. Visualize forthcoming events on that stage—the sales presentation, the public-speaking engagement, the important dinner party. Vividly picture everything going perfectly.

When you are ready to return to your ordinary consciousness, count from 1 to 4, telling yourself that by the time you reach 4 your eyes will open and you will feel alert and refreshed.

After some practice, you will be able to reach deeper levels of your mind instantaneously. How do you do this? You decide on a signal that will recall the feeling of being deeply relaxed and in touch with own subconscious. It could be simply turning your eyes up toward your eyebrows, or repeating in your mind the word or image you used to reach the deeper level.

Benefits: *The deep relaxation involved in reaching your subconscious is extremely beneficial to your body and mind. Studies have shown its effectiveness in relieving high blood pressure, insomnia, and other stress-related conditions. By creating vivid, powerful images in your subconscious, you can achieve that which you desire. These methods have been used by thousands to:*

- Stop smoking
- Achieve ideal weight
- Improve health and well-being
- Become self-confident and successful

NOTE: What you should understand about reaching your subconscious:

You reach it by deep relaxation that slows down your brain waves. You then reach the "Alpha" level—the level of creativity, of intuition, the level at which you are relaxed but alert and able to use more of your brain effectively. At this level, suggestions are particularly effective. You can use this level to achieve—and to become—that which is truly for your benefit. You need only to desire it, believe it will happen, and expect it.

When you reach this level, you can manipulate its content—which may have been manipulating you. (Old fears and patterns of failure may have been stored up from childhood and may still be affecting your life and your relationships. Anger and resentment from one situation may be carrying over and spoiling other situations.)

When you reach deeper levels of your mind, you can do much to release old patterns and create more desirable ones. When you function at this level of the mind, you are completely in control; you can return to ordinary consciousness the second your attention is needed elsewhere. The more you practice reaching your subconscious, the better you become at it.

Remembering Numbers

Eddie, 49, a fanatic but not very gifted golfer, amazes his young wife by instantly learning important new telephone numbers, street numbers, etc. "My Eddie's a real brain," she tells her friends. "He hears a number just once and never forgets it—no matter how long it is." Eddie's

secret is to relate numerical sequences to par on the two golf courses he knows so well. For example, 4-3-4-5-4 is an even-par finish on the first nine at Clearview. Ones and twos are especially easy because they would be fantastic scores. Eddie, it must be confessed, relates high numbers (for example, 6-6-9-8-7) to his own recent achievements.

Memory is based on association. The key to remembering numbers is to relate new ones to those we already know. Most people know, or at least should know, the following:

- phone number (home and work)

- street address (home and work)

- zip code (home and work)

- social-security number

- phones of doctors and other emergency numbers

- phone numbers, street addresses, and zip codes of close friends, relatives, and business associates

Make a list of numbers like this you don't already know. Carry it with you and learn them whenever you are forced to wait. Then you are ready to do The Number-Joiner:

- Repeat the new number quietly to yourself 2 or 3 times.

- As you do, relate it to a numerical sequence you already know.

- The sequence does not have to match exactly. For instance, 4-2-1-7 could be your sister's street address with one subtracted from the last number.

- For "difficult to relate" numbers, look for some internal aid: Are some numbers repeated? Are they in sequence (up or down)? Mostly odd or even numbers? Multiples of 3? etc.

Benefits: *Easy, accurate recall of important numbers promotes confidence, efficiency, and success. You also save time by* *memorizing the key numbers to which you relate new ones.*

"If you can't beat numbers, join them."

Sharpening Your Powers of Observation

Someone runs into a psychology class, shoots the professor, and runs out. The professor falls to the floor.

A moment later the professor stands up again, says that the bullet was a blank, and asks the bewildered students to describe what happened. No one is able to give an accurate account. There is general disagreement about the description of the assailant, the nature of the weapon, even about the sequence of events.

This experiment is often cited to illustrate most people's limited powers of observation. These powers can be sharpened during a great variety of waiting moments.

- As you are waiting, become aware of your environment. Select the section of it that seems most deserving of closer scrutiny.

- Give yourself a limited amount of time—perhaps the time of one normal breath—to focus your full attention on the selected area.

- Turn away from it and try to re-create it in your mind with as much detail as possible.

- Examine the scene again to see how much you had missed originally.

As with most skills, the more you practice, the better you get.

Benefits: *Keener observation, promoting both pleasure and success. Alertness and precision of observation are essential qualities of successful people in all occupations. The better you observe and know your world, the more interesting it becomes for you, and the more interesting you become to others. It is a waste to go through life without a perceptive awareness of its variety, richness, and complexity.*

NOTE: If your are ever waiting with children, observation-sharpening can be turned into an entertaining and beneficial game: "Let's see who can notice the first dog (the first green car, the first person in a blue shirt . . .")

Waiting in Color

Dr. Fernley, a research scientist, has studied the effect of colors on mood and behavior. Some of his findings apply to waiting situations.

Wearing soft, mellow colors helps you feel more calm and relaxed when you wait. Blues, grays, and beiges are particularly good. Avoid wearing vibrant reds, oranges, and yellows. Although these colors may make you feel more dynamic and ready for action, they tend to cause impatience and irritability during long periods of enforced passivity.

When waiting for someone on whom you wish to make a particularly good impression, wear whatever makes you feel most confident and attractive. Your clothes should be comfortable but appropriate for the occasion.

What to wear while waiting for a job interview:

- For professional jobs, the business suit in conservative colors. Women should wear a conservatively colored suit, possibly with a brightly colored blouse. Green is not successful in business situations but thrives in a social setting.

- For service jobs, sparkling white tends to give a wholesome and hygienic impression. Waitresses report that a white blouse or top is often the most successful for landing the job.

- For women in all jobs, avoid brightly colored make-up that calls attention to itself on the face. You don't want to look as if you are hiding behind a mask.

If you wait a long time to fall asleep, it could be because the colors of your bedroom are too stimulating. For many people, blue promotes calm and relaxation. It is therefore especially conducive to sleep.

Colors affect your appetite. While you wait to begin a meal:

- *Red* stimulates the appetite. Hence the popularity of red-checkered tablecloths and red-toned décor in restaurants. Red plates can make food (the exception is rare beef) look particularly appetizing.

- *Blue* has a slightly depressing effect on the appetite. It may be helpful to dieters.

- *Green light* can make food appear much less appetizing. Desperate dieters may wish to buy a green light bulb and see all their food in its light.

The influence of color is especially strong in waiting rooms, which are best furnished in soft, mellow colors. Blues, beiges, and grays are calming and conducive to relaxed waiting. Rooms painted in bright, vibrant colors have been shown to increase impatience, irritability, and even aggression. Pink reduces aggression. Hopeful football coaches have been known to paint the Visitors' dressing room pink!
These color effects are interestingly in accord with Eastern teachings. For example, green is the color of the "heart center" (located in the middle of the chest). This is the center of love and healing.

The color associated with the solar plexus is a bright lemon yellow. Someone who radiates vibrant energy is seen, according to Eastern teachings, to be operating from this center.

Bright orange light is seen as radiating from the center located two to four inches below the navel. Besides functioning as the body's center of gravity, this is the source of sexual-energy vibrations. In "sexy" people this center is quite active. (This is why being "sexy" has less to do with appearance than with considering oneself sexy. Consciousness triggers vibrations, and vice versa.)

At the base of the spine is a center said to radiate a bright red light. This energy center is involved with our survival and security instincts.

Scientists are now considering electromagnetic sensations as connected with light and color and as interrelated with various glands. (The ancient system of energy centers is related to the major glands of the body.)

Benefits: *Color bypasses the conscious mind and speaks directly to the emotions and the subconscious. It can be a valuable tool—*

both for controlling our own moods and feelings and for influencing others.

NOTE: According to some experimental work now in progress, blue light helps reduce fever, red light stimulates the circulation, and yellow light aids digestion. Green light is reputed to be conducive to deep and healing sleep.

WAITING

Special Situations

In the Grocery Store

John, 33, often shops for groceries after work. While standing in line at the check-out, he practices creative waiting.

Use your grocery cart for isometric exercises:

1. With both hands on the sides of the handle bar, pull sideways in opposite directions. Then try to push your hands together.
2. Alternate loosening and tightening your grip on the bar.
3. With both hands on the handle bar, push down with one hand and up with the other.

Remember to keep breathing naturally.

Benefits: *You tone and strengthen your upper body, arms and wrists. No one will know you are exercising.*

To avoid becoming frustrated in a slow check-out line:

- Try to estimate the amount your groceries will cost.
- From the content of other people's carts, try to picture their

life styles. By examining their figures and postures, you may be motivated to improve yours.

On the Tennis Court

Steve, 17, has been amazing the tennis pros. He is suddenly beating seasoned players and winning tournaments. Steve used to be just another nervous high-school kid, but now he is frequently breaking his opponent's serve. What's made the difference? Taking a deep, full breath while waiting for his opponent's serve.

He concentrates on inhaling deeply into his abdomen and feeling the energy of the breath spread throughout his body. Then, as he slowly exhales, he releases all his tension and is able to concentrate in a positive, relaxed way. At that moment all that exists for him is the ball.

Benefits: *Increased relaxation, concentration, and more effective use of energy.*

NOTE: If you observe basketball players before a foul shot or golfers before an important putt, you will often see them take a deep breath. Yogis, Sufis, Taoists, and other Eastern masters teach that slowing the breath and concentrating on it focuses the mind and energizes the body.

At the Office

J. D. LeBaron, 58, president of a large corporation, practices on his office rug every morning until he sinks three 10-foot puts in a highball glass. Then, while waiting to leave for lunch, he does Standing Push Ups against his desk.

1. Stand 3 to 4 feet in front of your desk. Rest your hands on the edge, shoulder-width apart.

2. Keeping your body in a diagonal line with no arch in the lower back, slowly inhale and bend your arms.

3. Lower your body in a straight line, as if it were a flat board.

4. Exhale as your arms straighten. Keep you abdominal muscles working.

You may only be able to do one or two at first. It is better to start by doing one correctly, adding one more each day as you get stronger.

Benefits: *Tones and strengthens your upper arm muscles and upper body. Any stable piece of office furniture can be used for this—a photocopier, file cabinet, etc.*

Drying Nail Polish

Vivien, 27, a model, does shoulder and arm exercises while waiting for her nail polish to dry. Do several of each while sitting or standing:

- Stretch both arms straight toward the ceiling, pulling up from the waist. Keeping arms straight, lower them slowly sideways.

- Raise both shoulders up toward your ears. Drop them.

- Roll shoulders forward, then backward, in circles.

- Extend arms sideways from shoulders. Make large circles first in one direction, then the other.

Benefits: *Good for posture. Improves tone and flexibility of shoulders and arms. Before you know it, your nails are dry.*

Recovering from an Illness or Injury

Glenda, 53, hotel-chain executive, became seriously ill. She then amazed her doctors with the speed of her recovery. These are some of the things she did while waiting to get well:

- Visualize yourself healthy and strong. Frequently concentrate on this image.

Then either:

- Picture yourself surrounded by brilliant white light like sunshine on fresh-fallen snow. Feel this light penetrate every cell of your body, healing, strengthening, and rejuvenating you.

Or:

- Use an ancient Eastern healing technique. Visualize yourself being drawn into the sun. Feel it absorb you.

Medical doctors are becoming aware of the effectiveness of positive suggestion and healing imagery. Researchers have been "discovering" the close relationship between body and mind. The medical practices of many primitive societies are based on this interrelationship, and so are the health-promoting exercises of Buddhists, Taoists, Yogis, Sufis, and other Eastern masters.

Glenda also recommends the following:

- Think of everything that goes into your mouth as healing and strengthening.

- Look upon your illness as an opportunity to do something

positive and creative: get a well deserved rest; examine priorities and values.

- Laugh a lot. This is a good time for humorous books, movies and TV.

Benefits: *A speedy and pleasant recovery, improved health, and decreased susceptibility to further physical problems.*

Warm-ups Before Sports

George, 36, an accountant, hated to keep anyone waiting, and he was late for his tennis game. He went straight from his car into a vigorous singles match. Five minutes later, he pulled a shoulder muscle.

Now that he can play again, George always warms up. While waiting for others to arrive, he does exercises. But even if he himself is late, he does at least some of the following:

- Walk briskly for a few moments.
- Jog lightly in place.
- Shrug to loosen shoulders.
- Loosen up arms as if shaking water off fingers.

Go through some of the motions the sport requires: swing a racket or golf club, for example. If your waiting period is long enough, you can get additional benefit from the following warm-ups and stretches:

Shake-outs

- Bend from the waist and let your upper body hang loose. Shake your shoulders and arms. Come up slowly.
- While standing on one leg, shake out the other.

The Swinger

1. Stand with feet together, arms reaching straight up. Feel that you are being pulled up from your waist.

2. Then swing your arms forward, down toward the floor and behind you, bending your knees as you do so.

3. Swing arms back up as your knees straighten. (Do this gently if you have a weak back.)

Knee lift

- While standing, raise one knee, grasp it and pull it towards your chest, and shoulder. Hold for a few seconds. Then do the other knee.

Leg-backs

- Place hands straight ahead on a wall, keeping feet 12 to 18 inches away from it. Stretch one leg back, pressing heel to ground. Then do the other leg.

Benefits: *A warmed-up body is less susceptible to injury, more relaxed, and more likely to perform effectively.*

Waiting to Play Well

A famous golfer visualizes each shot from start to finish before he makes it. Mentally he sets up the ball, swings, sees himself hitting it, and sees it going exactly where he wants it to go.

Champion skiers, boxers, basketball and football players, gymnasts and weight lifters are on record for visualizing in precise detail their movements and the success of their efforts. This process of visualization, they say, aids them not only mentally and physically but also emotionally.

Benefits: *Releases nervousness and tension.*

- Improves ease and precision of movement.

- Improves speed and quality of learning.

- Increases motivation and competitive alertness.

NOTE: By visualizing your sports performance in advance, you draw on a secret as old as the culture of ancient Egypt and as new as the latest championship event. Your mind is a powerful tool; this is one of its seldom fully utilized, yet readily available resources.

Losing Weight

Dr. Terra, a wise and motherly hypnotist, has great success helping people with weight control. She states:

> Most diets fail because they are based on self-deprivation, which threatens two of our most important feelings—that we are special and that we deserve good things. Self-gratification promotes these feelings on the subconscious level, so we stuff!

What does she advise? Don't just deny yourself. Instead, anticipate the problem during waiting moments, when you can plan to solve it in a variety of ways based on "delayed gratification." If possible, earn the pleasure while you wait—and perhaps even substitute a less-fattening reward. For example, anticipate that you will crave the remaining piece of chocolate cake. Plan that you will exercise for at least fifteen minutes when the craving arrives. You will then enjoy the pleasure even more because you have anticipated it longer and because you have earned it. You will also enjoy knowing that your exercise has burned off at least some calories. Still better, plan to substitute some other pleasure for the cake, such as a low-calorie movie or a delicious but lean restaurant meal.

Here are some of Dr. Terra's specific suggestions:

- Eat slightly less for several meals until you "earn" the calories of a treat you are postponing.

- Exercise briefly before you eat. Exercising actually does diminish the appetite—particularly if it is of short duration and right before a meal. (The liver releases the stored glycogen, which elevates the blood sugar.) A 5-to-10 minute session on a miniature trampoline is ideal.

- Half an hour before each meal, drink a small glass of fruit juice. It raises your blood sugar and takes the edge off your I-could-eat-the-furniture hunger. Grape juice works particularly well.

- While waiting for a meal, eat plenty of fresh raw vegetables.

- Chewing raw celery well uses up more calories than you are consuming, yet it satisfies the urge to chew and takes the desperate edge off your appetite.

- While waiting for your meal, take a moment to relax as deeply as you can and program your subconscious. See yourself enjoying and being satisfied with moderate portions, eating slowly, chewing thoroughly, and savoring every bite.

"If you still find it difficult to lose weight," Dr. Terra adds, "it may be necessary to look at some patterns in your life—patterns that involve some basic attitudes toward yourself. You can use waiting moments to examine these patterns."

- Is food a substitute for something missing in your life? Do you feel unloved, unfulfilled, or bored? If so, go after the real thing: better relationships, fulfillment of desires and ambitions, interesting and enjoyable activities. This solution is neither quick nor easy, but understanding the problem is a valuable first step.

- Is food a protection from something difficult or painful to face in your life? Extra food—and the layers of padding it creates—are often used as insulation against feelings of guilt or inadequacy, or against problems with one's own sexuality, or against the destructive power of someone else's negative emotions.

- Are you overweight because an overweight self-image is imprinted on a deep level of your mind? If you believe that diets won't work for you, they will be less effective. Your mind is so powerful that it can actually determine whether that hot fudge sundae will stay on your hips or be turned into energy and processed out of your body. One of the main values of a diet and exercise program is the message of slimness and attractiveness that is sent to the subconscious. Dr. Terra's advice: "Visualize yourself as slim—and everything you eat as making you slim, healthy, and attractive. Involve all layers of your mind in this visualization." (See "Program Your Subconscious.")

- Or is the problem simply that you are not motivated enough to do something about your extra weight? Part of you acknowledges that you need to lose weight, but another part doesn't really care enough. A mind divided against itself does not accomplish much.

Dr. Terra has found the following approach especially effective for women who need motivation to lose weight:

- Shop for clothes in a store where there are mirrors in the dressing room—preferably the three-way kind. Strip to your underwear and take a good look at your body. What you see in the unkind florescent light will strengthen your motivation.

- Find the perfect dress—in the size you wish to be. Don't buy it. Promise yourself that you will come back as soon as you lose the weight.

- Think about the dress every time you eat. Anticipate the pleasure you will have trying it on and having it fit your new, slim figure.

Benefits: *Lower weight, higher self-esteem, and pleasures you can be proud of. You experience none of the ill effects of self-deprivation.*

Walking Your Dog

Knowing that he did not have much longer to live, Emma's husband gave her two poodle puppies. When he died, she had to sell the house and move into a new neighborhood, but the puppies were a happy distraction. They became her link with her new neighbors. While walking the little poodles, Emma made friends with other dogs and their owners. People from four to ninety-four came around to inquire, pet, and give advice.

Soon everyone noticed that Emma was carrying little books on her walks with the poodles. They discovered that she had a collection of booklets on trees, flowers, birds, and insects. While walking her rambunctious poodles, she began to identify various flora and fauna by looking them up in these booklets. She delighted the neighborhood children, who now consider her a living encyclopedia.

While taking your dog for a walk:

- Make new friends or get to know old ones better. Even sophisticated suburbanites tend to drop their masks and open their hearts when they see an appealing pet. It's a good moment to make genuine human contact.

- Learn about the aspects of your environment that people often fail to notice. In addition to flora and fauna, you can observe everything from architecture to weather conditions.

Benefits: *As you use the time spent walking your dog to discover new things about your surroundings, you bring pleasure and benefit to yourself and to others.*

Being interested makes you interesting.

Before Meals

Dr. Vine, a famous nutritionist, declares: "For efficient digestion there is no better attitude than gratitude!" While waiting for a meal to begin, she advises, spend a quick moment counting your blessings. Enjoy the appearance and aroma of your food. Anticipate savoring every bite.

Benefits: *Tensions leave your body and mind. You are less tempted to gulp or overeat. Your food provides greater sensual and emotional satisfaction. Your digestion improves.*

NOTE: If you feel angry or upset, wait until you can develop a more positive and appreciative mood. You will enjoy your food more, and it will give you greater benefit. The ancient ritual of saying grace before meals has positive effects on body, mind, and emotions.

Giving a Good Party

Josephine gives fabulous parties. Her guests always feel particularly welcome and special. They leave beaming, and several have met their mates at one of her parties. How does she do it?

These are her suggestions:

- Get everything and yourself ready early and beautifully. Then study your guest list.

- Make a mental note of something unique and interesting about each of your guests. When you see them, they will sense the positive feelings you have thus evoked in yourself toward them. They will feel welcome and special. The best in them will come out.

- Plan what to say when introducing your guests to each other so that their conversations can take off. (Joe and Susan could sit next to each other during the whole dinner and not discover that they both bake bread or do amateur theatricals.)

Benefits: *Both you and your guests have more fun. Your party will sparkle as each person is encouraged to bring out the best in himself.*

On a Slant Board

Celebrities whose appearance is essential to their success use a great variety of practices and products to keep themselves youthful. The item you are most likely to find among their beauty secrets is the slant board. Some of the reasons they give for using it are:

- "Brings a glow to the face."
- "20 minutes on a slant board in the middle of the day is the equivalent of two extra hours at night."
- "A daily session on the slant board keeps you from ever needing a face lift."

Edna 28, a dental assistant, considered buying a slant board. Her apartment, however, was too small for one more piece of equipment. She considered propping up her ironing board, but it seemed like too much trouble at the end of a tiring day. She decided to use her sofa and some cushions.

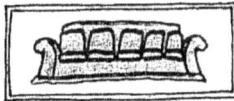

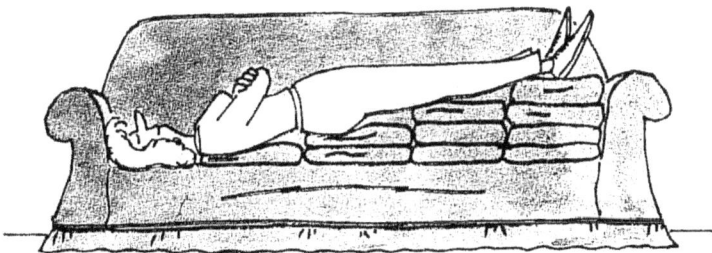

Four cushions under her feet, three under her knees, two under her hips, and one under her upper back gave her the perfect incline. She uses her creative slant board whenever she waits for her nail polish to dry.

- Determine what angle of slant and period of time works best for you. Most slant boards have an elevation of 15-24 inches.
- It is wise to start with a small slant for just a few minutes, and increase gradually.

Benefits: *Increased circulation in the face combats the effects of aging and fatigue. Your internal organs are refreshed from the reversal. It also revives tired, aching feet and relieves the discomfort of varicose veins. The slant board is effective for men, too.*

Exercises Behind a Menu

Antonia, 44, looks ten years younger and intends to stay that way. As a restaurant critic, she finds many opportunities to do facial exercises behind menus. She does only the relatively inconspicuous ones so that no one can catch a side view of anything unusual or alarming. Once, she let her menu slide down a bit and her hopeful escort, encouraged by her puckered lips, gave her an unexpected kiss.

While holding a menu over the lower part of your face and waiting for a waiter or waitress to appear:

- Say the word "you" to yourself with as much exaggeration of the facial muscles as possible. Hold for a few seconds while you try to stretch back the muscles on the sides of your face. It may help

to feel that you are trying to flatten your ears against your head. All this will lift and tighten the muscles around your cheeks and mouth.

- Press lips tightly together in a straight line and smile slightly. Hold for a few seconds; then make a small "O" with your mouth, as if puckering it for a kiss. This smoothes and tightens the mouth area.

- Tighten your jaw muscles; then relax them and let your jaw hang loose. (Much tension is carried in the jaw muscles. Relaxing them makes your face more attractive and your whole body more relaxed. You enjoy your meal more.)

Benefits: *Better facial muscle tone, increased circulation, and a more youthful, relaxed appearance.*

Cooking Breakfast

Janina, 70, has 8 devoted male admirers and incredibly beautiful skin. While waiting for her breakfast to cook, she always puts a masque on her face and neck.

- If she is cooking eggs, she puts the egg white that's left in the eggshell around her eyes, cheeks, mouth area, and neck. It's almost invisible, costs nothing and requires very little effort.

- If she has more time and is alone, she whips up one egg white in a cup with a fork, then whips in about a teaspoon of heavy cream. She spreads this mixture all over her face and neck (freshly washed in very warm water, so that the pores are still open). As her masque dries, she often adds more. The egg white and cream mixture can be kept for several days in the refrigerator and reused after a few whips with a fork.

- Either masque is kept on as long as convenient (twenty minutes is ideal). The face and neck are than washed with lukewarm water and moisturized with a good cream.

Benefits: *Smoother, lovelier skin.*

NOTE: Janina uses a variety of other natural substances on her face:

- *Aloe vera gel.* She takes a small cutting from the aloe plant she grows in a pot on her windowsill. (She talks lovingly to the plant as she cuts it, and the plant keeps thriving.) The juice or gel makes a wonderful skin-tightener and invisible astringent. It can be put on the skin morning and evening, right before the moisturizer. It promotes quick healing for burns and sunburn.

The beauties of ancient Egypt used it.

- *Avocado.* Whenever Janina is alone in the house while making a salad, she rubs a little avocado on her face and hands. It's rich in oil, protein, and vitamins, all of which are super for skin.

- *Cucumber.* Two slices are saved from her salad—to be put on her eyes as she lies on her slant board. They take care of under-eye puffiness.

- *Oatmeal.* The little that's left from breakfast makes a wonderful masque, either by itself or mixed with a little egg yolk.

- *Strawberry.* A slice makes an excellent cleanser for oily skin.

Waiting for Financial Gain

Larry, 34, a used-car salesman, finally put aside $6000 and called his friend Bob, a stockbroker. "The market's been rising fast," he thought. "I'll go for it." Broker Bob was enthusiastic too: "Most of the oils have had it, but there's this fast-growing little outfit called Gold-Medal Petroleum . . ." Larry bought 300 shares at $20 and began following Gold-Medal in the newspaper. In ten days, it fell to 16, and he called Bob. "The overall market's been a little sloppy lately," said Bob, "but Gold-Medal's got great potential . . ."

When the stock hit 12, Larry called Bob again: "They've all got to rest sometime, my friend." At 10, Larry panicked and sold out, switching into Zoomie Electronics at 9. "This one can't miss," declared Bob. It's been going up fast in a down market." Within five days, Zoomie had risen to 13, while Gold-Medal had fallen to 8. "That was close," thought Larry. "I might have stayed with that damn loser."

Three weeks passed. Zoomie retreated to 11, and Gold-Medal to 7. "I'm still better off," Larry decided. "And I've still got a profit." The next day, Zoomie failed to get a big defense contract that Bob had said was "in the bag." They stopped trading in the stock at 6.

That night, Larry did some serious drinking at Paul's Pub and ran into his friend Roger. Relating his woes, he suddenly remembered that Roger was supposed to be a successful stock trader. "Hey," said Larry as he finished his sad story. "I've heard you make big bucks on the market. How do you do it?" "Well," said Roger, "you've got to have patience. I'm an investor, not a trader. And you've got to go against the tide if you want to buy low and sell high." He leaned closer to Larry at the bar. "Right now, I'm accumulating a little stock called Gold-Medal Petroleum. Nobody wants it. Sold as high as 25 only last summer, and now it's down to 7 dollars a share. Forming a solid base there, though. And there's no change in the fundamentals—it's real value, not some high flier like Zoomie Electronics. Why, I think that within a year Gold-Medal could easily double, maybe even get as high as 20!"

Here are Roger's rules for investment. In his words, "It pays to wait":

- Wait before investing your money. Investigate to make sure the security represents true value.

- If the stock you want to buy has just risen sharply, wait until it "corrects" to a more reasonable level.

- If possible, try to time your purchase just after an overall market correction. As the market then rises, it will tend to pull your stock up with it—even if your stock still has a little downward momentum.

- You will hear lots of stocks recommended, and you can't buy them all. Wait until you hear a stock praised by at least two respectable sources. Then wait until it has fallen 5 to 10 percent from "recommended" level.

- Plan to wait at least a year before you sell. You will then avoid the high commission toll of frequent trading. Also, your profit will be long-term capital gain, which could result in a substantial tax saving. There is one possible exception to this: If your stock rises so sharply that the yield becomes very low and a correction seems almost inevitable, consider taking your large, quick profit. Then, happily gritting your teeth, pay the tax. But even in this case, greater profit may result from longer waiting.

Benefits: *Increased net worth, easier sleep, and peace of mind.*

Deepen Your Spiritual Life

Beverly, a high school teacher and busy mother of four, longs for a deeper spiritual life. Her entire day seems filled with work and family obligations. Her computer is a valuable tool, but she becomes frustrated by inevitable delays.

Some of her friends meet regularly to pray for the world. From them, she has learned that we each have a source of light within us, in our "Solar Plexus." When our hearts are filled with love, we can radiate this light to all that is. Beverly has also learned a new way to pray for her family, her friends, and the whole world, wherever people are suffering.

It is an ancient form of prayer taught by a New Age spiritual teacher. Beverly simplified it for use while waiting at her computer. "I'm connected to the world-wide web," she thought. "So instead of feeling irritated, I can become part of a "Spiritual World-Wide Web." This is her prayer:

- Let there be Christ Light throughout my physical body. Now my body is filled with this light.
- Let this light fill the room . . . this house . . . this town.
- Let this light pour forth to fill this whole country, all the people in it . . . all the people in the world. May the world be filled with this light.

Benefits: *Sending love, peace, and blessings to others has a way of rubbing off on the sender. Whatever positive and loving thoughts you send out have a way of coming back. As the old saying puts it:*

"What goes around comes around." This spiritual exercise tends to counteract self-absorption, while enhancing our awareness of our connection to all of life.

Postscript
....
CREATIVE WAITING

Do you ever have to wait in situations not described in this book? Be creative in adapting the suggestions to your own life. For example:

You spend 40 minutes every working day strap-hanging on a bus and subway.

- This is not in the table of contents, but you notice "Waiting in Almost any Situation."

- In that section, you find "Standing Isometrics" and decide you can do the first two exercises even if your hands are not free.

- You do the exercises several times whenever you strap-hang.

- This soon becomes almost automatic: you think of it as soon as your hand touches the strap.

You spend several minutes each day waiting to use a photocopier.

- You look through the section "Waiting in Line" and select a few exercises.

- You do these every time you stand in that line.

- After they become part of your daily routine, you add some exercises from "Waiting in Almost any Situation."

- Soon you find that you can combine exercises—for example, you can do some eye exercises while you raise and lower your heels.

You have lost your job and are looking for another.

- "Achieving Self-confidence" helps you to develop a healthy awareness of your own worth.

- You find suggestions under "Waiting to Meet or See Someone" about the attitudes and posture to assume for important job interviews. The ideas in "Avoid Nervousness" and in "Be Impressive" help you to present your best self.

You blow dry your hair and use a curling iron almost every day.

- Since you are looking in the mirror anyway, you decide that these are good moments for facial exercises. You find one in "Waiting at the Telephone" and another in "Exercises Behind a Menu." You also experiment with the "Invisible Face Exercise."

- Soon you also do these exercises in the situations suggested in this book.

- You decide that while you are holding facial contractions, you might as well contract the muscles of your pelvic floor, as suggested in "What Every Woman Should Do." Soon one exercise will remind you of the other, and you automatically and easily combine them.

Your job stresses and worries have been following you home.

- You turn to "Stress Discovered and Dissolved." As directed, you examine your body for tension—and release it.

- You also turn to "Relief From Tension" and apply it to your own situation. Riding home on the commuter train, you close your eyes and imagine yourself walking on a beautiful green field, with a deep-blue sky above. In your hand is a colorful bunch of helium balloons. Your boss's face is on one of them. Your office rival's is on another. Next week's evaluation of your work is on a third. You open your hand and watch them all float away.

Habit can be enslaving. But a good habit can be freeing. If a certain situation automatically suggests a certain exercise, your life becomes that much smoother and easier. And the feeling of success which comes from making progress on problems can also become habit-forming, giving you a sense of mastery over your life.

*You have the right to a beautiful and energetic body,
radiant health, a relaxed and attractive face,
and a peaceful inner life. Exercise it.*

APPENDIX

....

The Early Adventures of This Book

PERSPECTIVE: TOUR DE FARCE

From *The Washington Post*
Friday, April 13, 1984, p. B5, Style Plus

by Eleanor Rowe

My job, I thought, was merely to write a best seller. After that, the interviews would not intimidate me: I'm a survivor.

I grew up in Poland and Austria, among the horrors of World War II. As a 13-year-old immigrant, I read Dale Carnegie's *How to Win Friends and Influence People* and was irrevocably bitten by the self-improvement bug . . .

May, 1980. Everyone around me in the endless supermarket line seems bored, irritated, or drugged by gossipy tabloids. My book is conceived: I will show people how to use waiting time profitably and enjoyably.

Drawing upon 20 years of self-improvement from Aikido and belly-dancing to Yoga and Zen, I write the book. Accepted by Facts on File, it acquires the ambitious title *Waiting Games: How to Get Rich, Powerful, Sexy and Healthy While You're Killing Time.*

August 20, 1983. Hurray! *Reader's Digest* will run an excerpt from *Waiting Games* and even pay me $2,700.

August 25. A call from Detroit: Would I be willing to fly there for the nationally syndicated "Sonya Show"? Would I!

I meet an author currently on book tour. "Get some media coaching," he advises. "You see yourself on video cassette and learn how to handle tough questions." But it costs $600, which I'd rather spend on clothes.

September 18. "Book Country" fair, New York City. My publisher's booth is covered with blown-up illustrations from *Waiting Games*. One minor detail: The book is not available yet. Smiling energetically, I help distribute 2750 flyers which say "Come meet Eleanor Rowe, author of *Waiting Games*." Sample comments:

"That poster is a howl. Can I buy it?"

"Where are the books?"

"You know, stress is killing us all."

"I never wait."

"What can I do about my backache?"

September 27. Detroit, "The Sonya Show." Ten of us are crowded into the Green Room, awaiting execution. "This too will pass," I tell myself while doing breathing exercises. Suddenly a tense woman in beige walks up to me with, "How come you don't seem nervous?" Soon I am demonstrating relaxation techniques to the whole group. On camera I remember a line from Dale Carnegie: "Love your audience." Soon I feel an enthusiastic surge of energy coming back to me. Sonya's final words are, "You're delightful," and I float out of the studio.

October 2. *Globe* magazine phones. They want to do an article on my book. My book! A quick call to my publisher. "Oh, dear, didn't anyone send you a copy? Only a few came in, and they must have been sent out for publicity. Oh, and your editor took the rest to the Frankfurt Book Fair."

Many of my radio interviews are call-in talk shows. I can do them at my desk or, they tell me, in the bathtub. Several interviewers claim to have a copy of my book in front of them. Desperate to see it, I call my agent. A copy arrives by express mail. It exists! I take it to a Russian emigré cocktail party. The book elicits an occasional raised eyebrow: Anything aimed at commercial success evidently compromises one's soul. How much easier it is to share people's sorrow than their joy.

Telephone hookup with Providence, R.I. I discuss a frequently asked question, "How do you get sexy while waiting in line?" Then I tackle weight-loss and insomnia, still trying to provoke calls from the listening audience. Finally a call:

"On Main Street there is a store where you can get an owl."

"Where on Main Street?" my interviewer asks. Apparently this question had come up during the previous segment. If I ever need an owl I'll know where to go.

I map out a brilliant new radio strategy: I will declare that becoming rich, powerful and sexy is "a matter of mind, heart and garbage." That should get a reaction. But when I announce this on Miami radio, the interviewer immediately asks:

"How long did it take you to write this book, Eleanor?"

Hookup with Grand Rapids, Michigan. I carefully introduce "garbage" as the negative past experiences we all carry around within us. The next 20 cities are informed that it takes some people years of analysis to get rid of their garbage, but *Waiting Games* can help you for $6.95.

November 10. I'm waiting to go on a TV talk show in New York, trying not to be nervous. Since one of my messages is good posture, I sit erect. Three people rush over, hissing "Relax!" The atmosphere is strained, cold and efficient.

As the show begins, I launch into my "B-E-S-T way to wait" formula. "B is for Breathing deeply and slowly," I explain. "And E is for relaxing your Eyebrows. This releases the tension in your face," I add, gaining confidence. At this point, the lovely interviewer asks, with a celestial smile, how you can get rich while standing in line. Problem: how to switch gracefully back to "S is for relaxing your Shoulders" and "T is for standing Tall."

November 11. Books still not available. Calling several stores, I discover:

"It's not out yet."

"Sorry, we're sold out."

"I think I've heard of it."

"We'll probably get it in after Christmas."

And, finally: "Yes, we have four copies." I race to the store and finally find them—buried in the psychology section.

The fault lies not with my publisher, I learn, but with the distributors and stores, who push established authors during the Christmas rush. A desperate call to my agent, who does more of her magic. Soon I hear a major chain will carry my book after all.

Good news from the Frankfurt Book Fair: A British publisher bought the rights to *Waiting Games* for $1,800. It's also been sold to distributors in India and Australia. (Later I hear that it will be published in Japan, and I will get four copies in Japanese.)

November 21. My Midwest tour begins in Chicago, the morning after the nationwide showing of "The Day After." One interview is held in a restaurant-pub. Hunched over a strong drink, the fiftyish radio host asks to borrow my copy of the book. Scanning the table of contents, he begins the interview with: "What do you do while waiting in line after seeing 'The Day After'?" I gulp and reply: "Well, that movie makes you realize how precious time and life are. And of course *Waiting Games* helps you make the most of both." I now feel I'm doing all right without those $600 media coaches.

Back home, I have radio interviews all across most of the country, except for the Deep South, but the book still is not generally available.

November 28. "Panorama," Channel 5's TV talk show. I'm to be on with Famous Amos, the chocolate-chip cookie millionaire who's promoting his book and cookies. The topic: success. Jesse Jackson is waiting with us in the Green Room. Amos gives him a box of cookies, and Jackson waves it before the camera at the end of his interview. Meanwhile, I leaf through Amos' book: He envisioned only success and gave it his all. On the show we discuss his self-created luck as he rose from menial worker to cookie king. Amos later sends me a large tin of his cookies. It is one of the few good things my 17-year-old son sees coming out of this "weird" book affair.

I come home to find two minutes of heavy breathing on my answering machine.

December 2. Channel 4 Evening News at 5:30. In curlers in the makeup room, I'm given practice questions by the co-anchors. "We already know the answers," they say. "We just want to see how many minutes you take."

On camera, I do the "Vowel Howl" and some exaggerated isometrics with a grocery cart. I manage to keep from rolling the cart, and myself, off the edge of the small platform.

December 6. Boston. My live call-in interview is scheduled for 11 p.m. The taxi driver at the hotel assures me he knows where No. 3 Fenway is. "A 12-minute trip, lady." Despite the violent rainstorm, I try to relax . . .

After 40 minutes of blinding rain, five sets of wet directions and numerous examples of my driver's vocabulary, I call the station. It's at 3 Fenway Plaza, not Street! Soaked and breathless, I rush into the studio at exactly 11 p.m. At first the call-in questions are dull, but I'm suddenly amazed to hear the voice of an old friend. She praises my book while I try to keep a straight face. We discuss how to duplicate the ability of a well-known actress to transform herself at will from anonymous pedestrian to radiant, recognizable star.

Back in the hotel at 1 a.m., I call my friend to thank her and learn she has bought the only four available copies of *Waiting Games* in the Boston area. The 24-hour room service is closed for the night, but I get five hours sleep.

A TV interview is scheduled for early the next morning. Looking into the mirror at a haggard face, I decide on emergency measures. This time, room service comes through. I order oatmeal and a raw egg, mix the yolk into some oatmeal, and spread the mixture on my face. The maid barges in to find me upside down doing a shoulder stand with goo all over my face. She leaves, speechless.

December 26. The CBS Morning News! *Waiting Games* and I will be in people's homes from coast to coast. Four times my big moment had been postponed, to the consternation of friends and relatives across the country and the enrichment of AT&T.

Waiting on the set, I rehearse my answers. Though I had told the producer I could handle "almost anything," she gave me a list of practical, sensible questions. But when the cameras roll, these are not the questions I get. Morton Dean pleasantly asks: "How do you get sexy while waiting in line?" and "How do you get rich at a red light?" He also gives me some easier ones. Finally, he asks: "Ms. Rowe, if I read your book, will I really get rich, powerful, sexy and healthy?" My answer is:

"Aren't you all of those things already?" He briefly hesitates, smiles, and says: "You'll be back."